LANDSCAPE IN EMBROIDERY

LANDSCAPE IN EMBROIDERY

Verina Warren

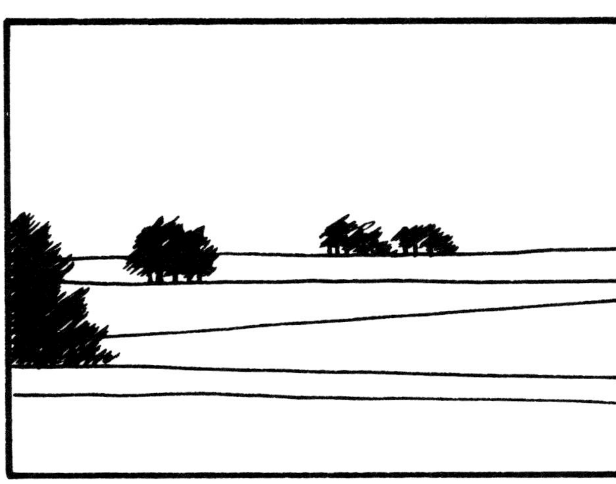

B.T. BATSFORD LTD
LONDON

ACKNOWLEDGMENT

My special thanks to Stewart Warren for his help and support during the writing of this book, and also for his expert photographs, and his technical advice and diagrams for the chapter on mounting and presentation.

I should also like to thank the following people: Mike Williams for his assistance and advice in the printing of the photographs, and for his excellent colour photography; all the people who have kindly allowed their work to be used in the book; and finally Sue Hadfield for her help in typing out the manuscript.

VERINA WARREN
1986

First published 1986

ISBN 0 7134 4567 X

Typeset by Servis Filmsetting Ltd,
Manchester

Printed by
Anchor Brendon Ltd,
Tiptree, Essex
for the publishers
B.T. Batsford Ltd
4 Fitzhardinge Street
London W1H 0AH

CONTENTS

INTRODUCTION

Asked by a friend how long a piece of work takes to complete, my husband answered promptly, 'Three weeks and twenty years' experience.' After the initial laughter, I thought about these words and decided that the remark was very astute. It does take years of experience to develop an art form. It is not only the techniques which one has to develop, but also a sense of awareness – a knowledge of one's media combined with the faculty of intuitive observation. It is in the art of looking that the difficulty arises.

We may all think that we do look closely enough at our environment. We can appreciate a sunny day without any difficulty, but how often have you noticed the change in light and colour of the sky throughout that day? Have you observed the sunlight shining through the leaves of a tree, casting patterns of light and shade, varying in its intensity? And have you seen the same light cast deep shadows, dark in tone and hue?

Most probably you would enjoy a sunny day for its brightness and warmth, which make you want to get out and enjoy the fresh air. But would you really notice the sky's vast expanse of blue, coloured in washes of fading tone, or see the creamy-white petals of the moon-daisy amongst the sun-perfumed grasses? Next time such a day arises, go out into the countryside and observe the details of your surroundings; do not take notes – just look and enjoy.

Learning to observe the landscape around you is the essence of this book, because observation is the foundation of design and it is the mechanics of design which cause so many embroiderers problems. This is a truth I have encountered in many day-schools and lectures, where the very term 'design' seems to create a mental block or transports well-adjusted people into moods of despair. New techniques can be learnt with ease, so why not design?

The misconceptions arise from a lack of understanding amongst the untutored. It is felt that unless an art course has been undertaken, then the mysteries of design remain forever locked to the unenlightened.

Although some forms can be complex, the basics of design can be understood and learnt, and it is easier to grasp that knowledge if your powers of observation have been developed. So 'looking' at landscape opens up a new thought-process which helps you to step more easily into the intricacies of design.

I tutored a design course in America where students ranged in age-group and ability. All were extremely enthusiastic and willing to learn; that willingness is an essential part of learning. Talking to a group of students about tree shapes and structures, I mentioned the old adage of looking at the shapes between the branches rather than at the tree itself. I was astounded to discover that many of them had never heard of or considered this well-known formula.

The following day they arrived for the class, full of amazement at the new awareness they had discovered in looking at the patterns made by the negative shapes of the spaces between the branches. One lady informed me with delight that she had nearly crashed her car while looking at all the trees on her route home; she had never realized how many different shapes could be found.

Although I do not advise you to look for shapes while driving, I would suggest that if you've never looked before, you try this simple exercise. The patterns formed by the negative shapes can be most interesting.

The design section of the book, Chapter 3, covers different aspects of design, explaining some of the principles, such as the use of line or structure, and

relating them to everyday instances. There are series of exercises for you to carry out, showing, for example, how from a simple shape such as a square, a more complex design can be achieved.

The chapter then goes on to consider the use of design and materials, introducing texture to the exercises, and finally considers design in nature. This section gives examples of line, shape and pattern found in landscape; these examples are only suggestions and their most important function is to encourage you to look for yourself, to see with your own eyes patterns of land, sea and air which surround you.

I have mentioned design exercises for you to carry out; these exercises run throughout the book and if followed in consecutive sequence, they will help to ease you through some of the more difficult aspects of using landscape as an inspirational source of embroidery.

The book also covers aspects of colour, beginning with the simple mixing of primaries (red, yellow and blue) and progressing to the more complex shades of tertiary colours. The exercises are designed to develop your sense of colour, encouraging you to mix shades rather than to use them straight from a tube. They relate to colour in the landscape and show how different seasons have different colour identities.

However representational or abstract your style of work, you can, by the application of colour, suggest the hour of the day or the season of the year. You can create dimensions of time and space, depth and infinity, on a surface of silk,

'Grey-green grass and flowers of gold, through windows high are seen.' The central section is a sprayed silk fabric, machine embroidered in whip stitch, with an inset of flowers painted in acrylic. This process is reversed in the outer arches, where the landscape is painted in an acrylic wash technique and the insets hand embroidered in free cross stitch.

because colour can give the illusion of a fluid and ever-changing scene.

After the abstract interpretation of colour, the technical sections show how to use the theory, giving instructions on painting and spraying and the examples of the effects which can be obtained. The use of stencils is described, and how they can be utilized for spraying landscape backgrounds.

The chapter on machine embroidery deals with certain techniques applicable to the landscape designs. It shows how to set up the machine for free embroidery, giving information on the equipment needed.

Machine embroidery is a particularly suitable medium for translating landscape into embroidery, as it allows for great detail with the ease of drawing. Surface textures can be built up freely and with speed. Many people are attracted by the medium but find difficulty in controlling the machine. However, with a little practice and perseverance, the technique can be learnt. I have spent the last 20 years mastering and perfecting the technique and adapting it to my own style of work. Even so, I still sometimes make mistakes, such as forgetting to put the presser bar down, which results in a tangle of threads under the machine. So take heart; mistakes will be made but they can be overcome and the technique offers so much freedom.

Where I have introduced a technique, I have shown the mechanics of the stitch and its relevance to interpretation into landscape design by the use of colour and texture, demonstrating its ability to 'draw' controlled lines, such as flower petals, or to give surfaces of texture suggesting fields or foliage. The final exercises are for your own interpretation of a subject using design, colour and machine embroidery.

Mounting and presentation is an important but often underestimated part of your work. Bad presentation can ruin an otherwise good piece of embroidery, so care is needed both in the choice of mount and in its assembly.

My own work is mounted and framed by my husband who works in partnership with me, and I am most grateful to him for all the technical advice he has given for this chapter. Step-by-step instructions show how the procedure is carried through to a finished result. A professional finish needs the correct tools for the job, so advice is also given on this, from steel cutting edges and craft knives to the choice of mounting boards or matts. It is stressed, however, that if you feel incapable of cutting a satisfactory mount, you would be well advised to take your stretched work to a professional framer.

Throughout this book, techniques and exercises are given for you to practise the skills suggested. The techniques are related to their use in landscape or seascapes, but remember that all techniques stem from that initial process of observation, which once learnt can be carried with you always.

1 *Inspiration*

Inspiration is considered by many to be a process of mystical illumination enjoyed by the few. It conjures up pictures of the artist, brush poised, waiting for visions. I agree that inspiration comes from within, that it is a strong, elemental force about which we have little or no understanding, but what is often not emphasized is that inspiration is the *idea*. How you translate that idea, in terms of inventiveness and sheer hard work, into a finished embroidery, shows the depth of your originality.

The idea or inspiration can come from many sources and landscape offers a wide choice of subject matter. There are many facets of shape, pattern and colour to be found in the country or by the sea.

A problem arises over how clearly you observe your source of inspiration. You may be fired with enthusiasm by the sight of a beech tree in its full autumn glory; but you must observe its position in the field, its overall shape, the formation of its leaves, its depth of shadow, how the tree stands in relation to others in the field and if darker greens enhance its brightness; otherwise your initial excitement may be lost when you are unable to translate the idea onto paper.

Observation gives clarity to inspiration and working directly from nature enables you to retain the initial freshness and vitality of the scene when transposing it into fabric.

CHOOSING A SUBJECT

Your choice of subject matter will determine the outcome of your finished work, so you need to think carefully about what really interests you. If, for instance, you love expanses of openness and want to exploit that special quality in your work, then the interior of a wood would not give the emphasis you seek. Rather, flat stretches of landscape, open moorlands, marshes or fenlands, and of course the sea are subjects which suggest a sense of space *(1)*. You can exaggerate the illusion of space with vast open skyscapes dominating the scene, or show flat landscapes disappearing into infinity, whereas the interior of a wood relates better to areas of intimacy and detail *(2)*. These are extreme examples but they do illustrate the point that subject matter needs to be carefully chosen.

The panoramic view gives a wide, unbroken sweep of the countryside. Stand on a ridge and look over the valley to see the landscape stretch before you and you will be aware of the undulations and contours of the scene; notice where light and shade move over the surface, reflected perhaps in the winding rivers or streams.

Parts of the scene, such as the valley floor, may be lit with sunshine, which brightens and enhances the colours within its light, but at the same instant this very brightness in the valley can throw the hillside into shadow.

These contrasting tones of light and shade give interest to the landscape and can be used to bring depth to your design, especially if the light and dark areas are later emphasized. For instance, darker patches of trees will intensify the shadowed hills while the sunlit areas can be enhanced by colours of bright clarity.

The same scene can look totally different in winter, when the hills and raised

1 *Open moorland has a spacial quality.*

2 *The interior of a wood has an intimate feel, which lends itself to detailed work.*

3 *Field shapes can form an abstract pattern of geometric shapes. Take special note of the variations in size and how field boundaries, such as stone walls, enclose and emphasize the shape.* (Photo: Mike Williams.)

ground may be covered with snow. This lightness over the hills would add contrast to the cooler blue-greys and browns of the valley where snow has not fallen.

With the panoramic view, it is important that you are aware of the *total* scene; you are capturing its essence without putting in every small detail. You must select the important features; look for the main groups of trees and the overall shapes they make; do not draw in each individual tree, or you will clutter the work and direct emphasis away from the panorama of the scene.

You will become more aware of the pattern of the fields, of their shape and size *(3)*. Those in the foreground appear larger and you will see details of objects. Bright patches of flowers will be intense in colour and the fields will be of a clearer hue. Some may be lighter than others – perhaps golden cornfields or recently cut meadows, pale green-beige in colour. These light-toned areas will be predominant in the landscape and you may wish to make a feature of them in a later design. As the scene fades into the distance, the fields will look smaller and give the illusion of merging together. Colours will lose their intensity and outlines become softened and blurred, shapes indistinct. The further the landscape recedes, the less detailed are the objects within it, while the colours change nearer the horizon, adopting shades of grey, blue or soft purples, depending on the time of day or the season of the year.

Although you will be aware of pattern and shape in a winter landscape, heavy falls of snow can flatten out contours, creating new shapes and areas of space. Hill lines can become indistinct, seeming to merge into the sky, while the snow reflects the surrounding colour. It is very easy to make the mistake of painting everything white, but this characteristic of reflected colour on snow can easily be seen. For instance, if the sky is leaden the snow takes on a greyish hue – it looks flat and cold. Trees and hedgerows, fences and walls, are predominantly shades of brown and grey. Patches of ploughed earth may be visible beneath a thin covering of snow in contrast to areas where it has been blown or drifted into sculptural shapes of opaque depths.

Alternatively, on a bright sunny day, a winter landscape sparkles with tints of silver and blue. Shadows look almost navy, while coniferous trees stand tall, in shades of dark blue-greens. The sky is often a bright, luminous blue, a colour which is reflected over the landscape, vibrant and clear.

4 *A cornfield showing foreground detail.*

5 *As a landscape recedes into the distance, outlines become softened, colours less intense and objects less detailed.*

6 *A winter landscape. This design shows a balance between opposites — light and dark, dawn and midnight. Machine embroidery is used to capture bare trees, which contrast with the flowers of summer. Thread-wrapped vertical and horizontal bands give structure and balance to the design.*

7 *Flowers in a border can be used to emphasize a season.*

8 *Dried winter grasses.*

Early evening winter skies are, to my mind, particularly beautiful: shades of pale turquoise layered with soft lilac and pinks, casting deep rose shadows on the snow before turning to midnight blues.

Colour can be used to suggest a season. Blues, for instance, are cool colours and work well in winter landscapes. You do not have to show a tree with bare branches to represent winter; a tree shape worked in blue can just as easily give the same illusion.

It is relevant at this point to discuss the different ways of interpreting the same scene in a different season. You can use colour to suggest a theme, rather than obviously duplicating a falling leaf or every opening bud. Take a tree shape within a field, changing only its colour, not its composition or shape. Spring is represented as a pale, leaf-green tree in a light green field, whereas a darker green tree against a grass-green meadow echoes the colours of summer. The autumn tree is depicted in russet or golden tints, perhaps in a field of pale ochre, while a blue tree in a grey-brown field suggests the cool tones of winter.

This type of approach can be developed to a more sophisticated level of design. Not only has each season its own colour range, but the plants and flowers pertaining to that season can be introduced to give added emphasis. You need only give a colour impression of these flowers for the illusion to be created: primroses in spring, foxgloves and buttercups in summer, wild berries in autumn, while winter claims the dried cow parsley, beige-grey and laced with frost.

The hilly landscape poses a different problem. Your subject matter will be more dramatic, with a greater emphasis on light and dark contrasting areas. If you are drawing mountains you will be aware of the sheer volume of their mass, giant structures of solidity. Their forms may overlap, giving dramatic stretches of dark tone and density. Their presence will dominate the skyline and if you are giving focal attention to the mountains, the proportion of land to sky should be greater, thus emphasizing the soaring peaks and strengthening the shape of the silhouette.

The linear characteristics of the landscape will be more obvious and these lines can be used to great advantage in order to strengthen the forms and add emphasis to rocks and crevices, by drawing in downward-sloping strokes and outlining strong shapes *(9)*.

The colour scheme should be more intense than in the panoramic scene, using red, purple and grey tones to achieve maximum effect. The top of each ridge or peak should be darker to differentiate it from its neighbour and give the whole mass a three-dimensional quality.

If you wish the mountain range to appear brooding and dark, do not add unnecessary detail to the main bulk, but keep the surfaces stark to emphasize the linear structure. Restrict the addition of trees to the base slopes, keeping textural detail to the foreground.

Mountainous areas can look very benign on warm, sunny days, especially when reflected in the still depths of lakes and tarns. Fast-moving rivers or streams would reflect broken colours and images which could be echoed on the land by patches of bright heathers or tall clumps of reeds.

Hilly landscapes have softer contours than those of mountainous regions; they are rolling rather than rugged and the colours are softer with perhaps more forestation of the slopes *(10)*. The hillsides could change from moorland to farmland, from open spaces to cultivated fields and meadows.

Perhaps the hills surround a lake or loch, rising from the clear waters. Along the shoreline boulders and rocks are strewn, interspersed with patches of encroaching green. As the hills rise upwards, trees follow the contours, growing sparsely amongst the rock faces and boulders near the water's edge, then regrouping into open copses and finally becoming woodlands. In this situation you would be more aware of the tree's structure the lower down the hillside you looked. Moving your eyes upwards, you would notice the lengths of the tree trunks before they finally disappeared under a mass of foliage.

If portraying fells or moorlands, try to capture the sweeping quality of the rising ground by keeping your lines bold and fluid; diagonal lines give a sense of movement and vitality, and if used in colour they could emphasize a sense of wind-blown bleakness *(11)*.

Try to get a feeling of movement into your sky, especially if you wish it to dominate the hills or moors. Wind-blown clouds, broken and dispersing, changing colour from light to dark, brilliant patches of sunlight in an otherwise overcast sky, slanting sheets of rain or snow – all help to give movement and drama to the composition *(12)*.

9 *This interpretation of a hilly landscape shows a greater proportion of land to sky.*

Flat landscapes have their own particular attractions. Often the quiet beauty of a simple scene is best suited to this type of treatment, perhaps concentrating the eye towards an old gnarled tree, a water-meadow full of flowers beside a stream, or a wide, meandering river banked by willows.

Trees in particular lend an impressive element to the foreground and add contrast to the flatness of the distant vista as in, for example, Constable's 'Study of Trees' *(13)*. Trees have such varied shapes, from the slender poplar or alder to the wide-spread beech, oak and walnut. Some have particularly distinctive features, such as the weeping willow's dense hanging foliage or the downward-sloping branches of the larch.

10 *A hilly landscape.*

11 *Dramatic use of sky in an open landscape.*

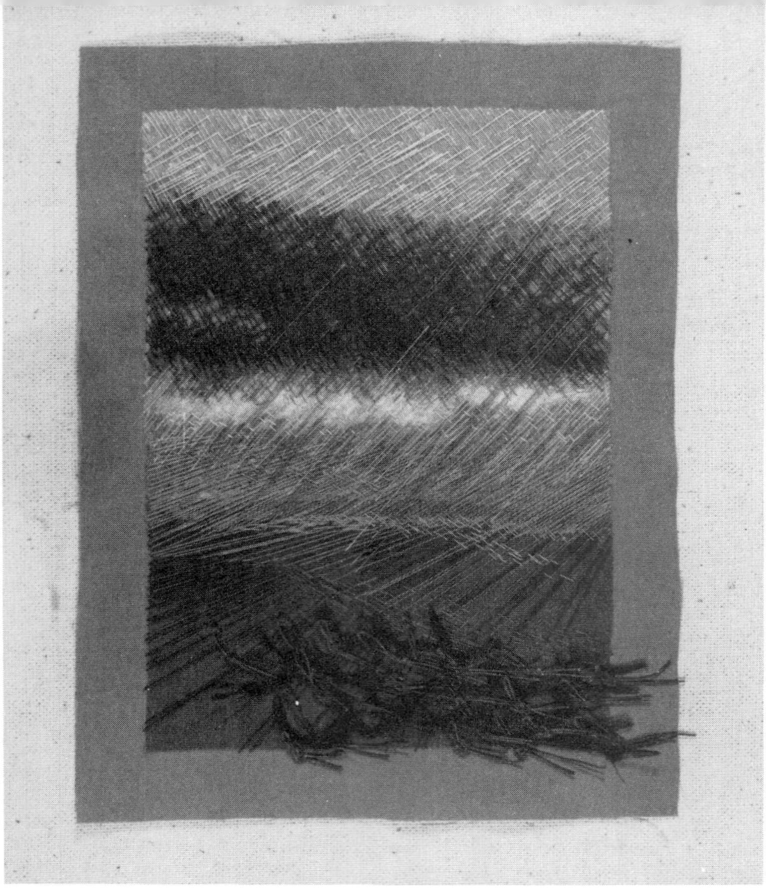

12 *'Moorland Rain', hand embroidery by Jean Draper. The background is in grey and brown cottons and transparent fabrics. The stitchery is in greys, beiges and white in very fine threads; cross-hatching in long and short straight stitches is used to build up texture. The foreground detail is in knotted scraps of fabric and linen thread.*

13 *Sketch of trees in Leicestershire, by John Constable.* (Victoria and Albert Museum.)

14 *In this design the trees are positioned so as to create awnings through which the landscape is viewed.*

13

15 *Within a flat landscape the patterns of a mown field give surface interest to the design and help to break up large areas of colour.*

16 *Spatial contrast between sky, land and sea.*

17 *'Valley on the Moors with Geese in Foreground' by J. M. W. Turner.*

The positioning of trees can make them more or less prominent in the landscape. They can give stature and loftiness if used in the foreground and extended high into the sky *(14)*. They can form canopies or awnings through which the landscape is viewed, or they can simply be used to create distance. They are also invaluable as heavy solid shapes casting dark shadows over sunlit meadows.

Flat areas can be given a greater impact by an inventive use of colour. They often stretch unbroken to the horizon, and lend themselves as starting points for abstract designs. Textures and patterns are more obvious on flat land, such as interesting ploughed fields where the lines of the furrows are curved or broken in one area and the burnt stubble in a cut cornfield is interspersed with shoots of new green grass *(15)*.

If you wish to emphasize the spatial quality of the view, make use of horizontal lines, stretching unbroken to the edges of the paper, to depict vast areas of grasslands. Give intimacy to this openness by taking a path through the waving grasses, letting it fade out before reaching the horizon. Place the horizon line below centre on the paper to give an illusion of expansion, so that the proportion of sky is greater than the area of land. Large areas of sky are more impressive when balanced against a flat landscape; this vastness seems to suggest infinity *(16)*.

The atmospheric phenomena found in the skies of Turner's watercolours show very well how the element of air can be best portrayed *(17)*. Notice how different weather conditions change the light and colour of the landscape, from soft, misty mornings or bright sunny days to the red and gold beauty of autumn sunsets. The time of day also affects the mood and colour of your scene and it would be a worthwhile exercise to sketch the same view at different times of the day, making notes on colour changes and shadow directions.

Seascapes give further opportunities for portraying natural elements, as they mirror the minutest weather changes. I often find seascapes amongst the hardest subjects to interpret, but if achieved they give the loveliest results. Nothing remains constant, as the entire scene is vulnerable to changes in the atmosphere. Clouds can quickly appear and sweep across a previously clear sky, changing the sea from sapphire to an unilluminated grey. The ocean can be imbued with a shimmering iridescence or emulate night's shadowy tones. It can appear smooth and glossy or rough and opaque, while the daytime haziness can change to silver moonshine. It is elemental, atmospheric and magical.

On a more practical level, there are certain difficulties to overcome, such as depicting waves way out to sea or crashing over rocks. Observe how dark shadows form beneath the crest before breaking, frothy and white, over rocks or shore. Follow the line of a wave and note how one section will break before the next; see how patterns form in the foam around the base of cliffs and note the wide, flat arcs forming arabesques on the sand as the tide advances and recedes *(19)*.

Shorelines can be smooth, with wide expanses of beach fringed by dunes, or rocky and wild with tall cliffs jutting out into the sea. Grasses and plants are sparse where vegetation meets sand, scattered clumps of waving grass or tall banks of reeds protecting the stray flower. Further inland sea pinks grow

19

18 *'Sea and Sky', hand embroidery by Jean Draper. Blue-grey and white transparent fabrics are used as a background to the straight stitchery which is carried out in very fine threads in a strongly directional manner to indicate the form of the clouds.*

19 *A design showing the changing line of a wave.*

20 *A seascape showing wide expanses of beach fringed by dunes.*

profusely amidst silvery-grey foliage. As well as the myriad details of the sea, fascinating textures can be seen in rocks, shells, pebbles, driftwood or seaweed.

Once the subject matter has been chosen, as much information as possible must be assimilated; this is an essential forerunner to design work.

Look at the landscape from different angles and positions and try to find the most interesting view. It is often advantageous at this stage to take photographs, because not only will you have additional information when in the studio, but just looking through a camera lens will limit the eye to a smaller area.

A card window-shape could be used if a camera is not available. This is a small piece of card with a square or rectangular shape cut out from its centre. Hold the card at arm's length and look through the window shape to select your subject. By doing this you are consciously making a design decision. Once you have found your angle of viewpoint, set up your drawing and painting equipment and survey the scene in front of you.

PAINTING AND DRAWING

I like to use watercolour at this stage, as I prefer the immediacy of the medium and also find it perfect for capturing hard and soft areas.

If you decide to work in watercolour, it is important to stretch your paper onto a board. Firstly, immerse the paper in a bath of cold water and let it soak for about five minutes. Lift out the paper, drain off the surplus water and lay the

21 *Detail of the seascape in fig. 20, showing the textural contrast between the drawn and embroidered grasses and sea pinks.*

22 *A design sheet showing different aspects of a view, and detailed information about it.*

23 *A watercolour of a snowscape.*

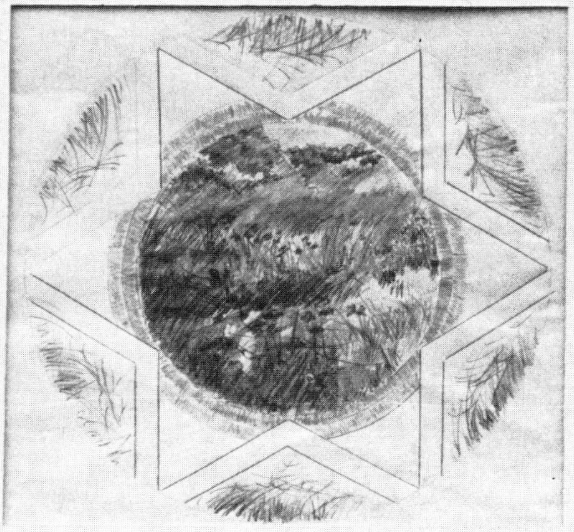

Waking Dra
based on S

24 *Sketches of fields showing various ideas related to horizon lines and textures.*

paper flat on a piece of board. Then secure the paper to the board with strips of brown sticky paper. Keep the board flat and let the paper dry naturally.

You can also use watercolour board or a good-quality watercolour pad. Do not use brushes that are too small or you will become involved in too much detail, too early. A size 14 brush is good for large areas of wash, sizes 8 and 5 for slightly smaller areas such as foliage, and numbers 0 or 1 for detail. I like to use tubes of watercolour paint, but you may prefer pan colours. You will also need clean rags for wiping your brushes and a palette for mixing the colours. An empty plastic bottle, rinsed and filled with clean water, is essential and is not as heavy to carry as a glass one. I also save plastic margarine tubs and use them as water jars or as extra palettes.

Other suitable media include waterproof drawing inks, used with pen and brush. The nibs come in various shapes and sizes, but an ordinary pen nib is perfectly good for the basic drawing, and a fine one is useful for detailed work. You can either do a straightforward pen and ink study, or apply colour washes of watercolour to the drawing when the pen work has been completed. Or you may like the free-flow formula acrylic paints, used in wash form. I prefer to use large brushes and make sweeping strokes, mixing the colour with plenty of water and keeping it as translucent as possible. I use watercolour techniques, adding detail last of all with a small brush. Acrylic paint dries quickly and one advantage is that it can be overpainted, so a small mistake can be erased. Care must be taken to ensure that all the paint is washed off the brush, otherwise the bristles will harden.

Alternatively, you could use pastel crayons, charcoal, or pencils, preferably with soft leads; I would suggest that you start with a 6B, a 2B and an HB pencil. If using pastel or charcoal techniques, remember that the finished result will be more of an impression of the scene rather than a detailed picture. Pastel crayons can be blended together to give subtle tones and soft edges. Charcoal marks can be smudged, a particularly good technique for depicting foliage, woods, clouds and anything which demands a soft or diffused outline. I would recommend that you invest in an aerosol can of fixative; you will then be able to fix your drawings when completed, thus preventing any possible smudging on the journey home.

Decide on an area of interest – perhaps a tree, a field full of flowers, or mist suspended over a valley. This is your starting point, around which you can work.

Put down on paper as much information as you can. It may be easier to draw lots of thumbnail sketches, rather than a detailed picture. Make colour notes if working in a monochrome medium such as pencil, as it is easy to forget actual shades. For instance, is the green field a yellow green, or does it contain a proportion of blue or brown? Perhaps it is a bright jade green. Be as accurate as possible, as this will help you when you want to plan colour schemes for your embroidery. Do not worry if your drawing is not very good; you will gain confidence as you progress and it is better to make mistakes now, so that they can be eliminated before the design stage. Regard this as an exercise, enabling you to record your own likes and dislikes within a given landsape.

Look at the horizon and relate it to your drawing. It could be a hard-edged, definite line, or perhaps it is broken by groups of trees, or softened by mist. Observe how the skyline lightens on the horizon, thereby defining the darker outline of hills or fields *(24)*. If trees or bushes break the horizon line, they can create solid masses, or they may thin out, to show glimpses of light behind.

You may find that only part of a tree line is visible if, for instance, the trunks are obliterated by a hillside. Look at the way hedges and walls follow the contours of the hills, or conversely how they dissect fields and land masses. It is interesting to note how irregular these areas can be. Paths, roads and rivers can lead the eye into the picture towards a focal point *(26)*. A focal point concentrates the interest, drawing the attention into the picture, towards the subject; this could be a pond or lake surrounded by tall grasses, a craggy rock on a beach, a group of tall trees, a cluster of farm buildings, or a bright patch of bluebells in a dark wood.

It is not always essential to have a 'subject', but if you are a newcomer to drawing and design, the process will be easier if you plan the picture around your theme. One rule to follow is not to place the tree, rock, or whatever is to be your subject in the centre of the paper. Move it to either left or right and slightly below or above centre. If you still feel unsure, roughly divide the paper into thirds and use one of the drawn verticals on which to site your object. In my own work, I have used the imprints left in a field by a tractor to concentrate the viewer's interest. Where the grass has been flattened along the tracks it became

25 *A tree line on a hillside.*

a different colour to the rest of the field *(27)*. I used this idea in the foreground of the picture to direct the eye along the track and into the distant hills beyond, giving depth and interest to the composition.

Consider the elements of light and shade, the direction of the sun and the consequent angle of shadow. Note also the balance of light and dark shapes in juxtaposition *(28)*. If a tree or hedge stands in front of a pale-coloured field, or has sunlight behind it, the foreground shape is visually thrown forward; it becomes more intense, the outline is stronger. Illusions of space and depth can be achieved by using cold and warm colours: blues in the background will give a recessive effect whilst warmer-toned colours such as ochre, rust and yellows give strength to the foreground.

Light and shade can create dramatic effects even if the day is misty. For instance, in mist the sun is pale but parts of a hill can be illuminated where the light breaks through. This effect can also be seen in moonlight, where the light appears brighter and features within the landscape take on an inky darkness.

Areas of intense colour can be related to more subdued tones: a patch of bluebells in a forest glade can suddenly be illuminated by a shaft of sunlight, giving very strong areas of light and dark.

26 *A path can be used to lead the eye into a picture.*

27 *Tractor imprints in a meadow direct attention towards the distant hills.*

28 *The shape of the tree is outlined against a pale field.*

29 *Areas of light and dark within a bluebell wood.*

30 *Light and dark areas give depth and density to this watercolour of flowers and grasses.*

31 *A watercolour showing flowers growing massed together.*

Note how the detail becomes more obvious in the foreground but fades to colour and tone, as it blends into the distance. If grasses and flowers are to be drawn, look at how they cross and bend, how darker areas throw forward lighter stems and give depth and density *(30)*. Grass is not always green and it doesn't always grow in vertical lines!

The wind creates movement in the grass, giving areas of light and shade with variations in colour. A similar effect occurs when rippling water reflects the light, breaking its surface into a myriad of colours.

Flowers are often found growing massed together; stems may not be visible and the blooms will touch and mingle, showing as patches of pure colour.

As you are observing and drawing, it is helpful to make notes beside the sketches. These will be useful when you are at home and cannot refer directly to your subject matter.

Although working from nature is my own preferred starting point, many people may feel daunted by the open landcape and that sheet of plain, white paper.

PHOTOGRAPHS AND ILLUSTRATIONS

If you do find it difficult to draw, an alternative source of inspiration lies in photography; you can either take your own photographs or use book and magazine illustrations. Use black and white as well as colour photography; monochrome prints can be useful later in the observation of shape and tone.

You should follow the same thought and observation process when taking photographs as you would when drawing, making notes to help you later. Take shots of the same scene from different angles, as well as many close-ups of relevant details. Look for the patterns and textures of nature: tree bark, lichens growing on stones and walls, pebbled shores, estuaries at low tide where rivulets of water run between mud banks. Fire breaks cut into forested hillsides give a patchwork effect, especially if deciduous trees have been planted with conifers, as different species show as separate areas of colour. Even in winter this colour difference can be observed.

Frost, ice and snow not only change the colour of the landscape but also create marvellous intricacies of pattern and texture. Photograph the design formed on the surface of a frozen pond or river, note how the structure of plants is changed as they stand stiff and frosted in the early morning. Look at the frozen patterns of grass; see if you can find differences between the grass in your lawn and that in a meadow or on a moorland. Look at the world in close-up, get down on your knees and photograph a patch of grass, viewing it as an insect would *(34,*

32 *'Delphiniums', by Richard Box. A panel of small pieces of applied fabric with some hand and machine embroidery.*

33 *Winter grasses, stiff and frosted in the morning snow.*

34 *Shapes and patterns found in a clump of grass.*

35 *Woodland grasses showing texture and linear movement.*

33

34

35), and then take a shot of the same patch from above, pointing the camera lens downwards. You could produce a whole series of photographs based on grass. Something so simple but common can be used as a source of inspiration for interpretation into a design *(35)*. That design can be as abstract or as representational as you wish it to be, but because you have studied its structure and form in great detail, your understanding of the subject will show through in your work.

Illustrations found in books and magazines can also be helpful as a starting point, especially if you can obtain more than one example of your chosen subject. Fields can be interpreted in many different ways. Try to find pictures of fields in close-up, or an open landscape composed of different-sized fields, and note how they are divided by hedges, walls, paths and rivers. Observe the difference in colour and texture between one field and its neighbour *(36)*. See if you can find examples of fields seen in different seasons; do the colours change with the seasons? Are there differences in the vegetation growth?

Do not always be satisfied with the first picture you find. Try to discover other examples of the same or similar subjects, build up a collection of illustrations and catalogue them under specific headings. When you want a design based, for instance, on flowers, you will be able to select examples from numerous illustrations. This selection enables you to think about shape and colour, to use the basic material as a means of developing your awareness. By doing this, your work will become a personal statement, not just an embroidered copy of someone else's photograph.

WORKS OF ART AS SOURCES OF INSPIRATION

In the past, many artists learned their trade by copying the work of established masters. They did this not to imitate another's work, but to extend their own techniques and gain knowledge in the process.

Sandro Botticelli, a fifteenth-century Florentine painter, shows in 'Primavera' and the 'Birth of Venus', his fine handling of linear patterns and delicate interpretation of nature, depicting a strong element of design and decoration.

Giovanni Bellini showed an observation of nature in the landscape backgrounds of his paintings, while the Venetian artist *Giorgione*, who was a pupil of Bellini, created a feeling of light and air, where the landscape became the real subject of the painting, not just the background.

Claude Lorrain was one of the leading landscape painters of the seventeenth century, a Frenchman who lived in Rome and studied the hills and plains around the city. His work was a realistic representation of nature but from it he selected chosen motifs to create illusionistic scenes.

Apart from Turner and Constable, who were mentioned earlier in this chapter, the other obvious artistic sources come from the Impressionist period, such as the work of *Monet* and *Pissarro*, who used a technique of pure and mixed colour which fuse on the retina to give a brilliance of sunlight and light, thereby creating an impression of a scene.

Georges Seurat used the technique of pointillism, in which small points of colour were used to build up the picture, with light and shade playing a great part in his work.

Cézanne attempted to see the world objectively, a style rooted in the nature of things, not in a subjective sensation. His work gives the impression of depth and distance with the adjustment of one area of colour to its neighbour; this results in an apparent breaking up of flat colour surfaces into a mosaic of separate colour facets.

Mondrian began as a landscape painter in the style of the Amsterdam Impressionists but his tree paintings (1908–16) show his progressive development from representation to abstraction. This series of paintings would be particularly useful to study before interpreting your own drawing into a design.

There are many artists whose work you may prefer, but my intention is to introduce to you the importance of looking and analysing and thereby responding to works of art. It is both interesting and enriching to visit local museums and art galleries to study the paintings and tapestries. See how other people have tackled the problems of composition, tone and colour; you may find it gives added inspiration to your work.

36 *Textures and patterns in fields.*

2 Design

CONCEPTS OF DESIGN

Planning a design is rather like planning a garden. The project is devised in the head, committed to paper, contemplated, revised, and finally solved. In the case of the garden, the end product is a glorious display of colourful blooms, but your thoughts, when put to paper, result in a distribution of line, shape, proportion, tone and colour, within a given frame of reference (without, of course, the hazardous complications of inclement weather).

Design can be one of the most difficult subjects to teach, or to learn, but the ability to design is inherent within us; the difficulty lies in the interpretation of the idea.

How often have your clear lucid thoughts melted into thin air when confronted with a sheet of plain paper, so that you feel unable to start, either through lack of knowledge or lack of confidence? Design makes a unique and personal statement, and although initially subjective, it is the clarity of objectivity you seek. Try to acquire an awareness of purpose in every mark made, coupled with an ability for self-criticism, and you will be preparing for yourself a foundation upon which you can build a structure, and within which your landscape can develop.

Line creates rhythm and movement. It gives continuity and progression, and can indicate position or direction. It is straight-edged and hard or soft and fluid, curved or angular.

Chinese and Japanese paintings show how line has been used to its maximum advantage. A single brush stroke conveys an impression of a petal falling from a flower, or a blade of grass growing and bending, all within the same movement.

Try to manipulate a mark through varying thicknesses, without lifting the brush from the surface of the paper *(37)*. Rely purely on the pressure of the stroke to suggest forms such as leaves, flowers, trees and waves.

Many different types of mark can be made with different materials: soft or hard brushes, brushes with rounded or stubby ends, long mobile bristles, pens, cotton-wool buds, strips of fabric, straws or fingers.

Different types of marks can be made by using different types of media – inks, acrylics, poster paints, watercolours – and all these can be applied in different ways, very dry or saturated, stippled or smooth. The line can be fluid, gelatinous, transparent or opaque.

Exercise 1

Try to devise as many linear marks as possible, using as many different media as possible.

Exercise 2

Take an empty jam jar and into this put an assortment of brushes, pens and pencils. The aim of this exercise is to draw, using line only, the objects in the jar *(39)*. You are not seeking a representational copy but are abstracting the image and seeing the *line* – the differences in thickness, length and density.

You can also try this exercise using natural forms, finding the linear structures on wood, leaves, stones, fingers or hair.

37 *Continuous marks of varying thicknesses.*

38 *Painted grasses illustrating the use of a simple mark.*

39 *An interpretation of brushes, in line only.*

40 *The use of line to suggest movement in a cornfield.*

Take it a step further by looking for the 'fixed' lines in landscape – telegraph poles, building structures, fences, walls and as many other examples as you can find. These simple exercises will help you to develop your powers of observation.

Line can also stimulate our imagination of movement when straight lines are used with curves. This creates a rhythm, which in turn represents the tossing of waves, or wind blowing through cornfields, rippling linear movements of curves and lines *(40)*. It can illustrate the movement in clouds, long and wispy over the sea's horizon, or scudding across stormy skies. Line can suggest rain and wind or depict sudden bursts of sunlight streaming through breaks in the clouds.

Although line can suggest all these subjective qualities, it still retains its essence of abstraction. For instance, when it is isolated, a linear mark is purely abstract and totally unrelated to anything else, but if you take that line and use it to outline a shape, it then takes on the appearance of a solid object; so line also helps to create structure.

Structure gives stability and balance; it can also be arranged to give a progression of pattern and shape, as in repeat designs on dress or furnishing fabrics.

The basic *spiral* illustrates growth and movement, as seen in plants twisting and bending around archways, tree trunks and branches. You can see examples of it in old tips and rubbish dumps, where vigorous plant growth has intertwined itself around rusting cars and old bedsteads – nature's regeneration in an urban and derelict landscape. Let us take, as an example, the convolvulus. Seen in a hedgerow it looks merely decorative but upon closer inspection, it is found to have numerous stems and tendrils, intertwining not only its own structure but also that of the hedge. Take a twig and look for the growth points, the points where the minor stems leave the main branch, and you observe an alternate, upward growth pattern, a spiral movement *(41)*.

The *circular* structure illustrates swirling movements, like those often seen in water, where ripples turn and circle in streams and rivers. Tides ebb and flow, leaving pools of water where eddies form circles in wet sand. Relating this theme to plant life, look, for instance, at the circular construction of the cow parsley, where the 'spokes' radiate outwards from the central stem *(42)*.

Stability can be suggested by the simple plane and pyramid shapes. The *plane* gives area and shape to a design, and also proportion and balance. Look into a landscape and see how many different-shaped planes make up an area of fields *(43)*.

Exercise 3

Take three simple planes, that is, three 2.5 cm (1 in.) squares and experiment in joining them together *(44)*. You can draw these on paper, or if you prefer to work in three dimensions, use card squares and see how many various ways you can discover of putting three planes together. Also try rearranging their positions.

Exercise 4

Take a large stone and draw the planes only, keeping it all linear. Take a tracing of the drawing onto another sheet of paper and this time, using monochrome only, shade in selected areas to give a three-dimensional image.

The *pyramid* shape gives stability, especially if the heavier, darker areas are at the bottom of the shape, with the lighter tones towards the apex. It can be used in the grouping of objects to form a balanced composition *(45)* by ensuring that the main weight of the design takes up more of the lower half of the picture.

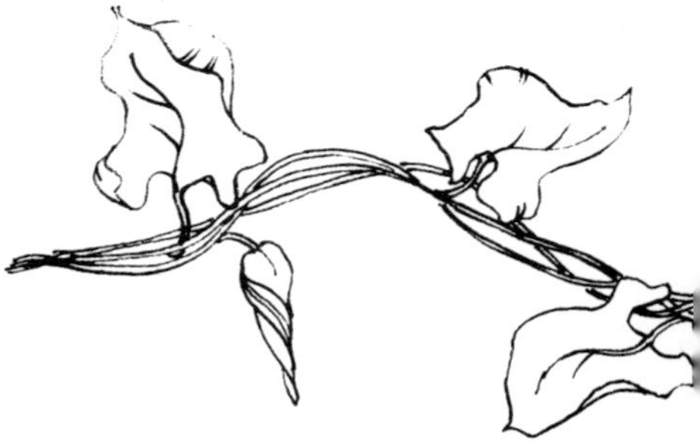

41 *An intertwining structure.*

42 *A circular construction.*

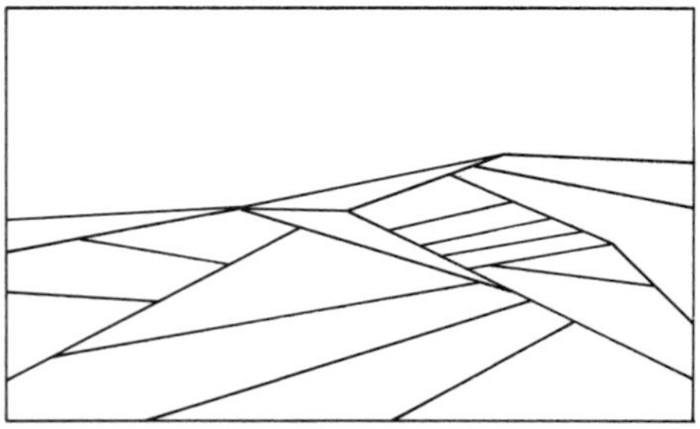

43 *Planes within a landscape.*

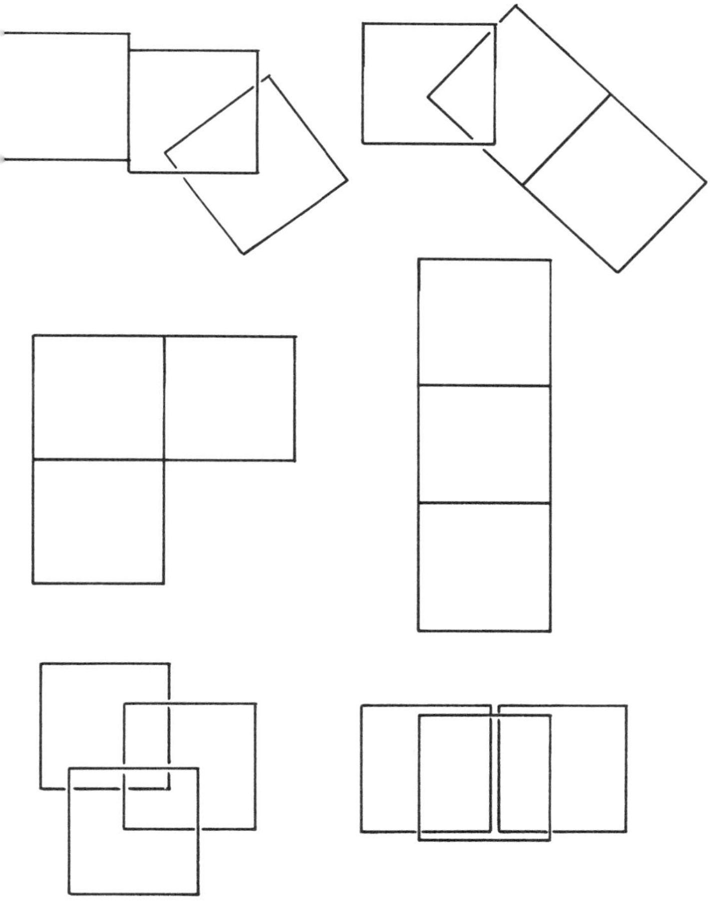

44 *Variations within three planes.*

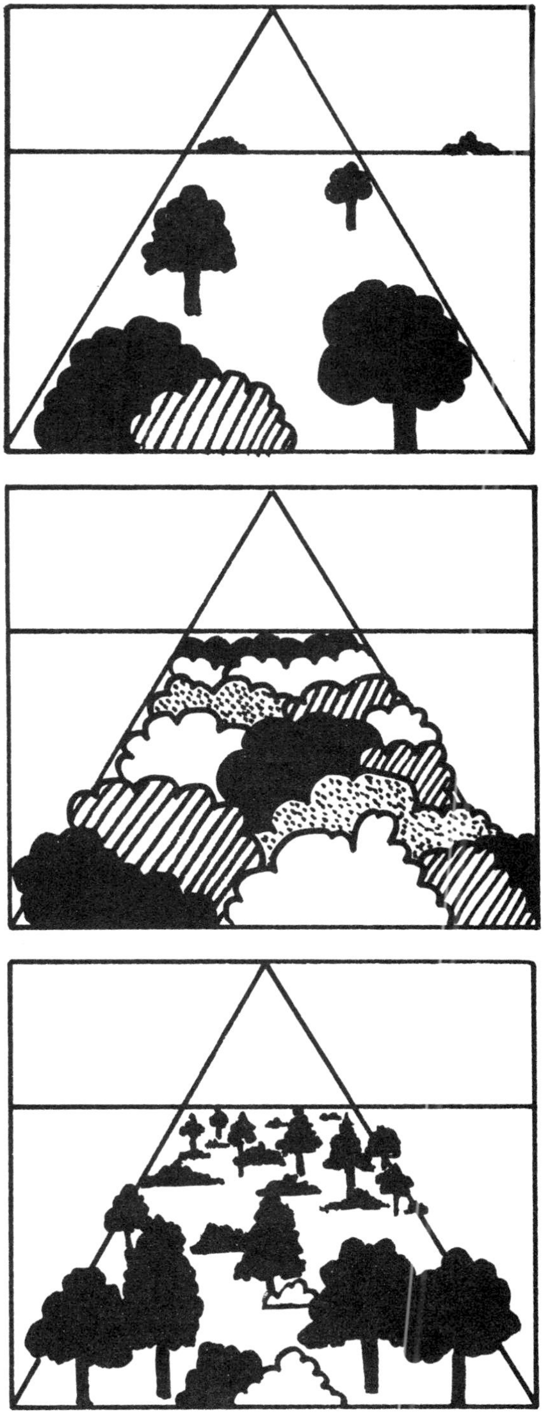

45 *Composition balance.*

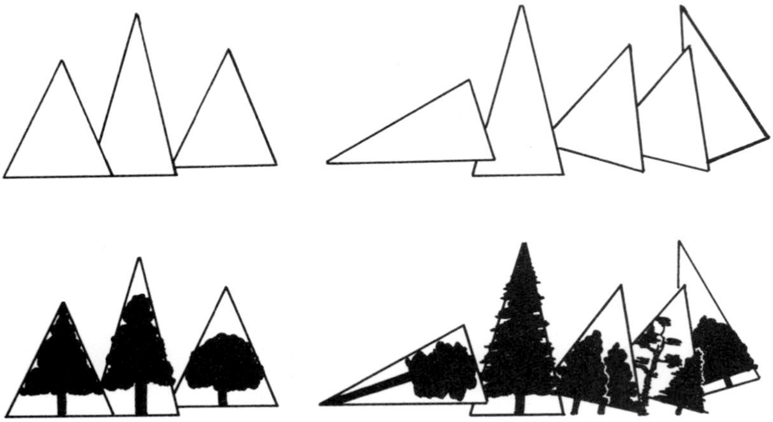

46 *Rhythmical balance.*

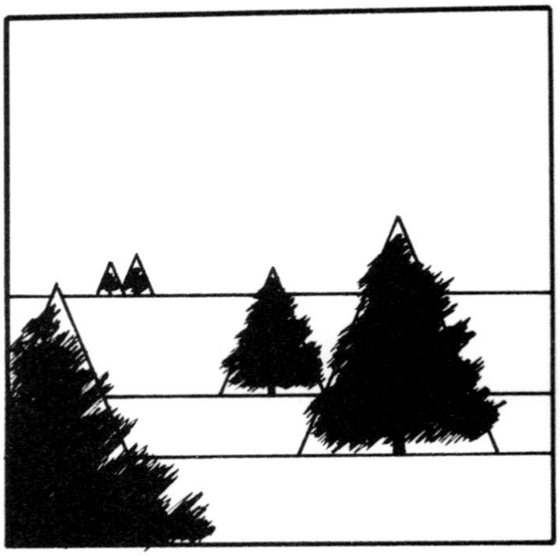

47 *Small triangles within the composition.*

Triangular shapes can also be irregular in size and can be used when positioning objects in a landscape. The repetition of a series of triangles of various heights, placed across the paper at different angles, gives a rhythmical balance *(46)*.

Smaller triangles can also be put within the main triangular composition, the most important element or focal point being the largest triangle *(47)*. Although the triangular shape has been illustrated for its balance and stability, it is not essential to keep the objects within the rigid proportions of the shape; by overlapping the contours, the relationship of the form is emphasized.

Perspective often appears daunting to the beginner, but a few simple rules can help to clarify the situation.

1 Objects furthest away from the viewer will have the appearance of diminishing in size.

2 The nearer sides of a rectangular object appear to take up more space than those furthest away.

3 A circular object will form an ellipse.

Parallel perspective Parallel lines in nature appear to converge on a point of the horizon, known as the vanishing point *(48, 49)*.

Angular perspective uses more than one vanishing point in the same picture. Lines at right angles to each other recede towards separate points on the horizon line.

Tone is represented by the distribution of light and shade, or by the pattern of light and shadow, giving a three-dimensional quality to the image. Light is fluid and changes its degree of intensity throughout the day. Observe light moving across a field and note how it intensifies the area of colour within its range, thereby dulling the tone of the rest of the field, now in shadow. One of the clearest ways of illustrating tone is to turn down the colour on a television set and note the various shades of black, white and grey. You can see how two colours, for example blue and orange, may look the same when seen in monochrome, illustrating the point that different colours of the spectrum can have the same tonal values.

Before we go back to drawing from landscape, I suggest that you try the following design exercises, as they will help you to understand shape, line etc. Use graph paper for all these exercises.

Exercise 5

1 Take a simple 5 cm (2 in.) square and divide it equally into three *(51)*. Look at the shapes you have made. Each area is equal in proportion to its neighbour. It

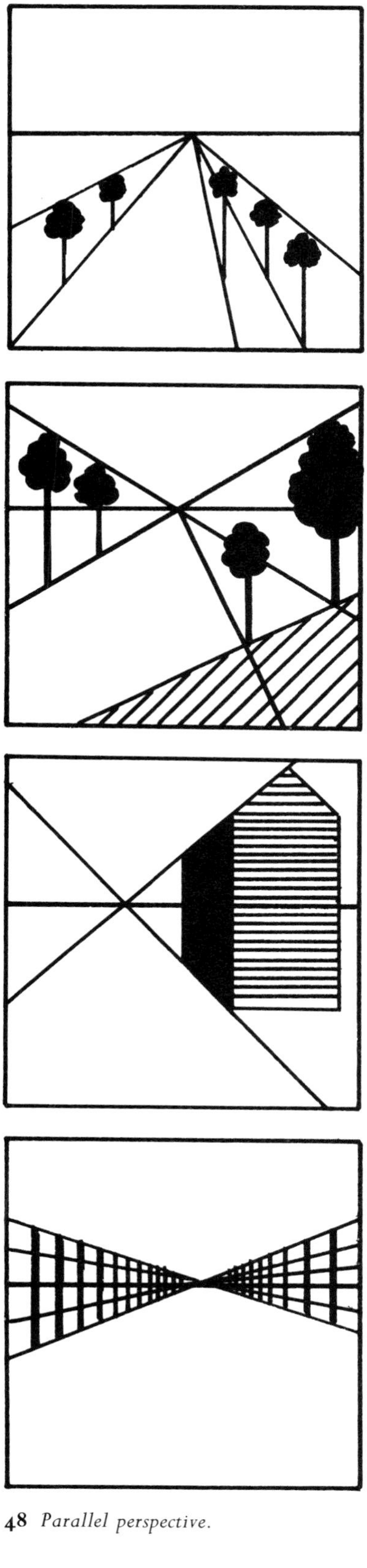

48 *Parallel perspective.*

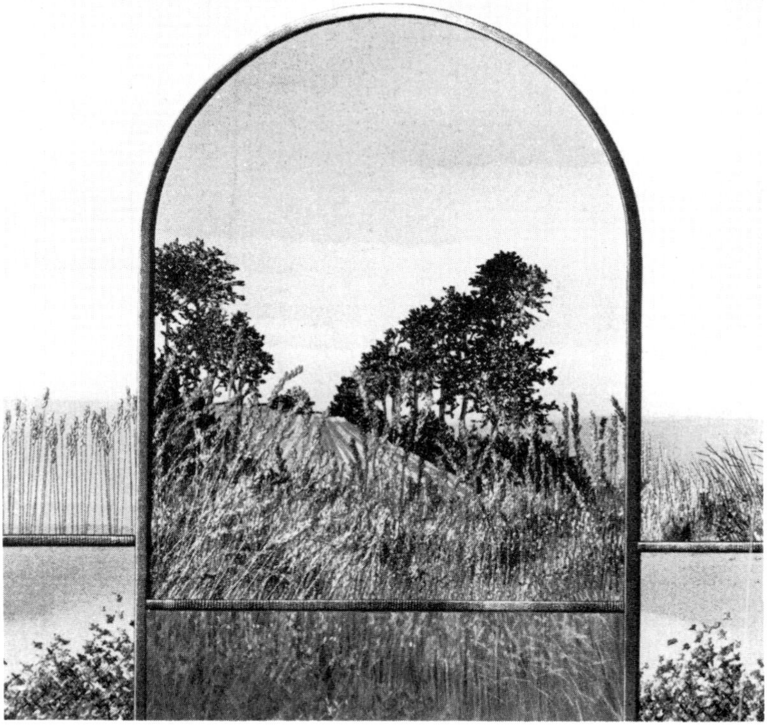

49 *Parallel perspective draws the eye into the picture by use of the receding tree line. This illusion of depth is further emphasized by the difference of sky tone within the arch.*

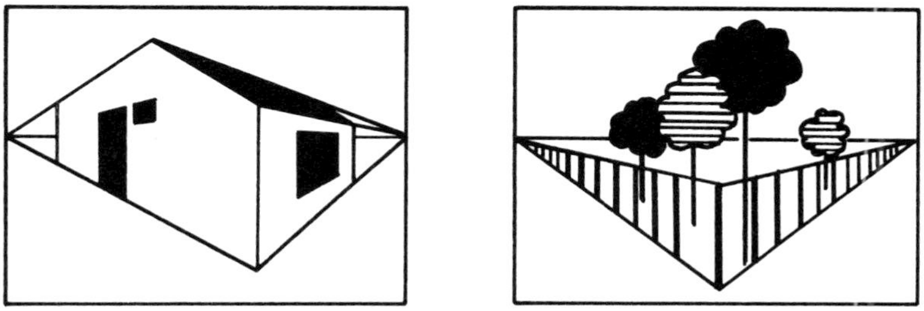

50 *Angular perspective.*

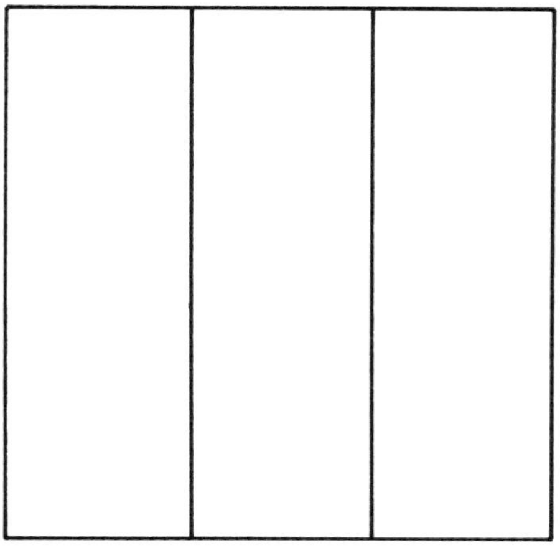

51

52

has no surface tension, the eye moves over it without interest; it is obvious and rather boring.

2 Now draw another four 5 cm (2 in.) squares. Working from left to right, divide the first shape into three by keeping the left-hand line in the same position as in *fig. 51* but move the other verticals further over to the right, so that the proportion of these sections is changed *(52)*. Immediately the balance is shifted; the square is visually of more interest to the viewer. It arrests the eye and has a more pleasing effect. Fill in the remaining squares using vertical lines so that the breakdown of the four squares gives a different proportion to each.

3 Draw another four 5 cm (2 in.) squares. Trace out the vertical lines from the previous exercise into the empty squares so that at this stage they look identical to the other squares. Now, dissect these lines with one horizontal. The horizontal lines will be in a different position in each of the four squares *(53)*.

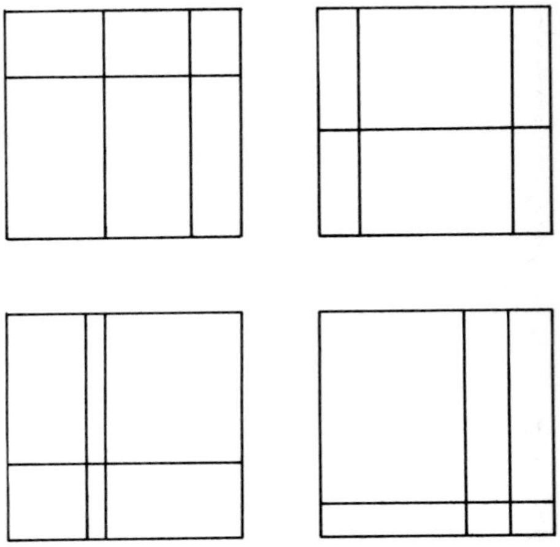

53

4 Add one more horizontal line to each square. Try to ensure that each new shape in this square is of a different proportion and that each shape is important and considered *(54)*.

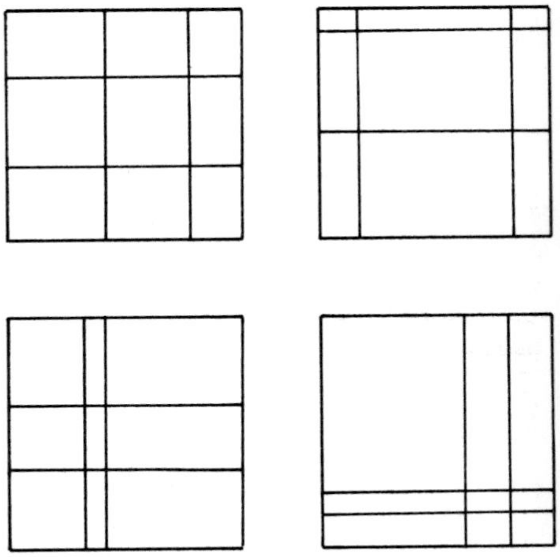

54

5 Extend this exercise by adding tone. Select three squares and in the first shade in two areas of tone, using shading of equal density. In the second square, shade in four areas and in the third, shade in six. These areas of shaded shapes must be carefully considered and balanced *(55)*.

Look at the final square. At the moment the shaded areas are all of the same density. Think hard about where you will put the darker areas; would a large shape, if darkened, appear too dominant? Do you want to space out the dark areas or group them together? When you have made your final choice, fill in three of the already shaded areas with darker tone until your third square contains white, shaded and dark shapes. Remember not to have all the corner areas of the same density, as they will be too similar and the design will lose its interest.

When you have completed the last square, cut out the shapes and try to rearrange them on a plain sheet of paper. Find as many permutations as possible and when you are really satisfied with one, stick it down onto the paper. You have now worked with shape, tone and line, so we will take this one step further.

6 Divide a piece of paper into nine 10 cm (4 in.) squares. Working from left to right across the paper, draw *(56)*:
(1) Three horizontal lines.
(2) Three vertical lines.
(3) Three horizontals broken by one vertical.
(4), (5) and (6) are divided by three fluid lines, although not all three lines need be the same length (think of hill lines).

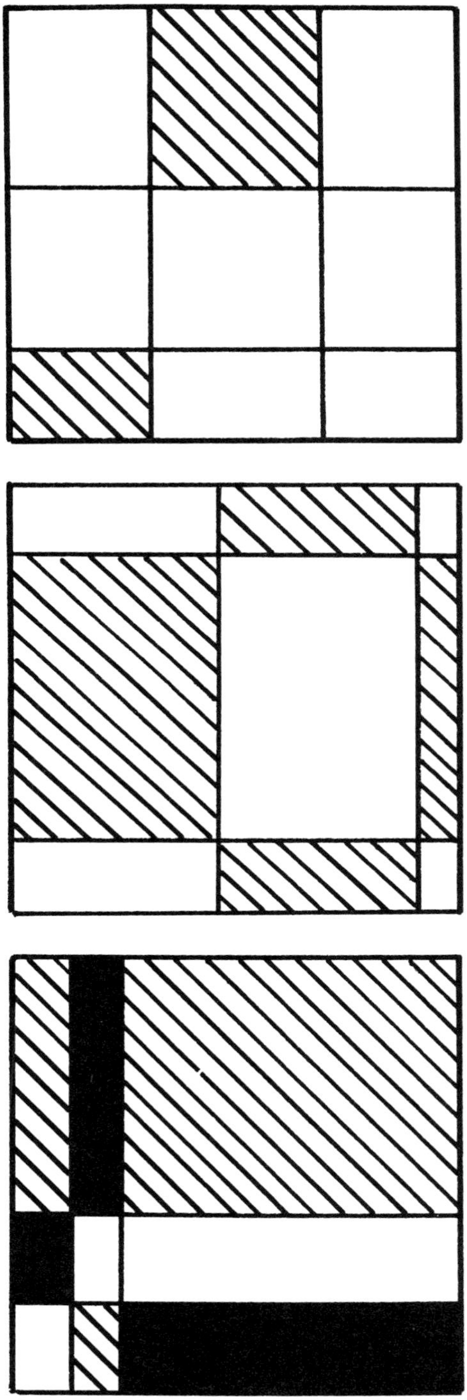

55

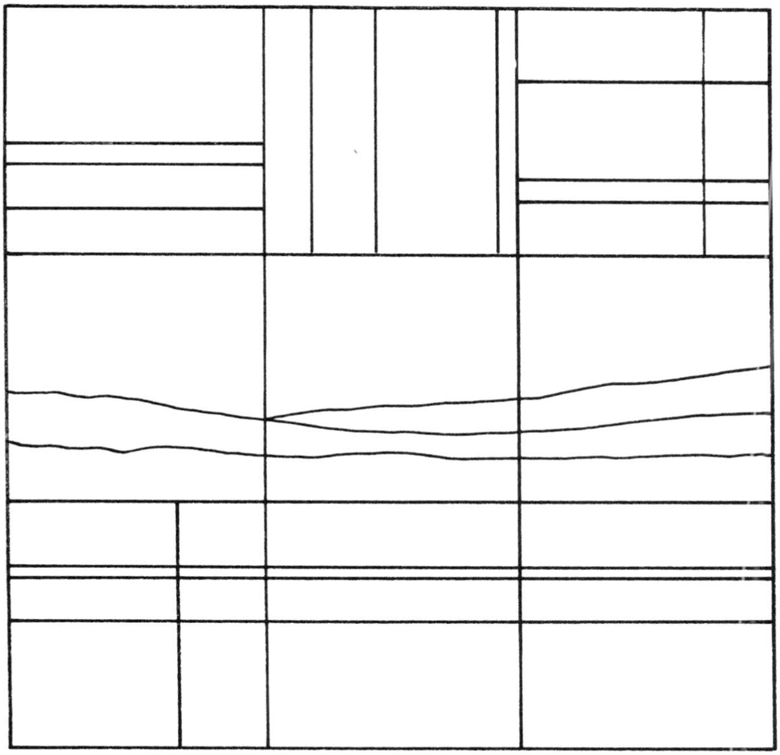

56

Looking at what you have already drawn, put into the bottom three squares the straight lines *you* think would balance up the design. In my illustration, I've added two long horizontals to connect the shapes and prevent the overall area from becoming disjointed. I then felt it needed one vertical to echo the lines in the top sections.

There is no limit to the number of lines you can put into the bottom three squares; this is your own choice – you make the decision.

Exercise 6

Using the monochrome design you have just completed, we will move on a stage further, by adding basic colour. I would recommend either designer's gouache or poster paint for this exercise and brushes no. 5 and no. 3. The three primary colours – red, yellow and blue – with the addition of white, are the only colours I want you to use, as we will consider colour in more depth in another chapter.

All that you need to know at the moment is that these colours, when mixed, will give a variety of shades:

> blue and yellow when mixed together gives green;
> red and yellow give orange;
> blue and red give purple;
> white will lighten the tones, e.g. white added to red will give pink.

Using no more than six colours (there can be different tones of one colour), paint your design very carefully. Think about the area and spatial quality of the shapes, for example dark shapes appear smaller while pale colours seem to enlarge the form. It is important to be aware of these modifications and paint your design accordingly. Leave some parts white and do not lose the basic grid pattern.

When this is completed, take a piece of paper or card and cut out a window shape 15 cm (6 in.) square from the middle. Place this on top of your painted

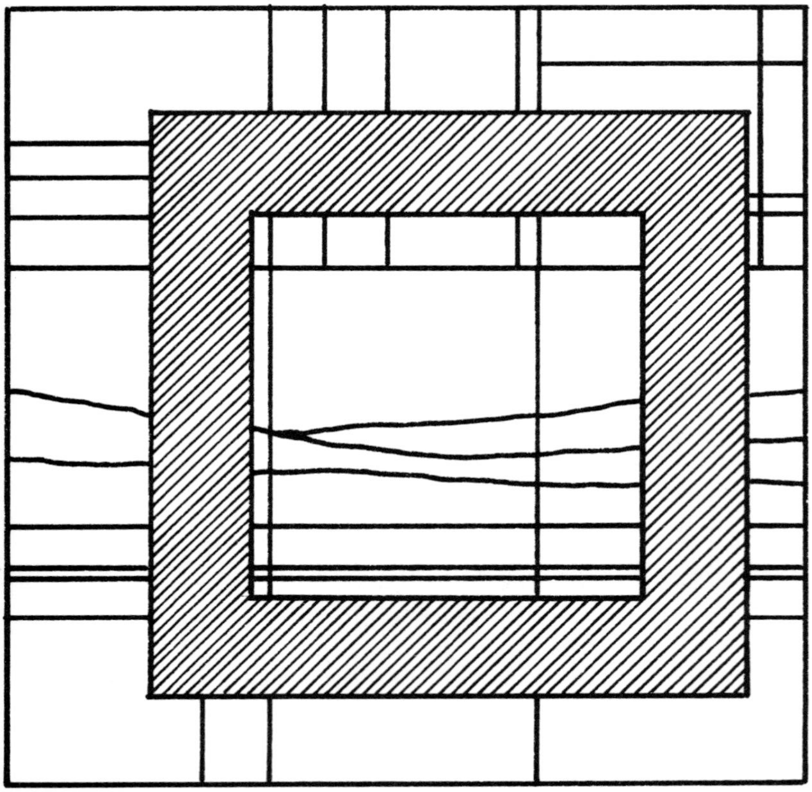

57 *Selecting an area of interest.*

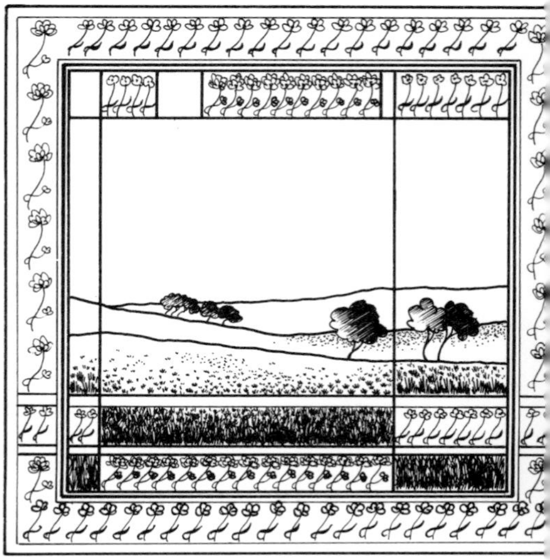

58 *The finished design.*

design and move it around the paper until you have selected an area you like *(57)*. Consider the shapes made by the window and analyse the proportion and line. When you are satisfied with the selected area, secure the window carefully with tape or drawing pins (thumb tacks) and, using tracing paper, trace out the pattern. Do not forget to draw in the outside perimeter lines of the 15 cm (6 in.) square.

Transfer this design, by gently rubbing over the back of the tracing paper with pencil. Take a clean sheet of cartridge paper and with the right side of the tracing uppermost, secure it to the paper. Carefully work over the traced outline with a sharp pencil, then remove the tracing paper. The imprint will be left on the paper underneath. Strengthen the outline by working over the lines in pencil. When this is completed, draw a 2.5 cm (1 in.) border all around the outside of the new 15 cm (6 in.) square.

Take a simple motif, such as a flower, and incorporate it into the design and the border. Use the areas of pattern in the same way as you used areas of tone, and with colour, build up an abstract design *(58)*. The motif you use could be in repeat, that is, a progressive repetition of the same motif. It could take the same form but be of a different scale.

If you still feel you lack the confidence of your convictions, and the thought of drawing in a pattern motif fills you with horror, you could alternatively use a sheet of wrapping paper, but choose one with a small print of a suitable scale for your design. Cut it up and stick it down on the area where pattern is required.

This is a time when you must think for yourself, using the framework of the design exercises to help you. If you are happy with the finished result you may like to carry it through into a small embroidery, using your favourite technique. However, the object of the exercise was to get you thinking progressively and to show how, from a simple, basic square, a design can evolve.

59 *Development of a motif to create painted and patterned areas.*

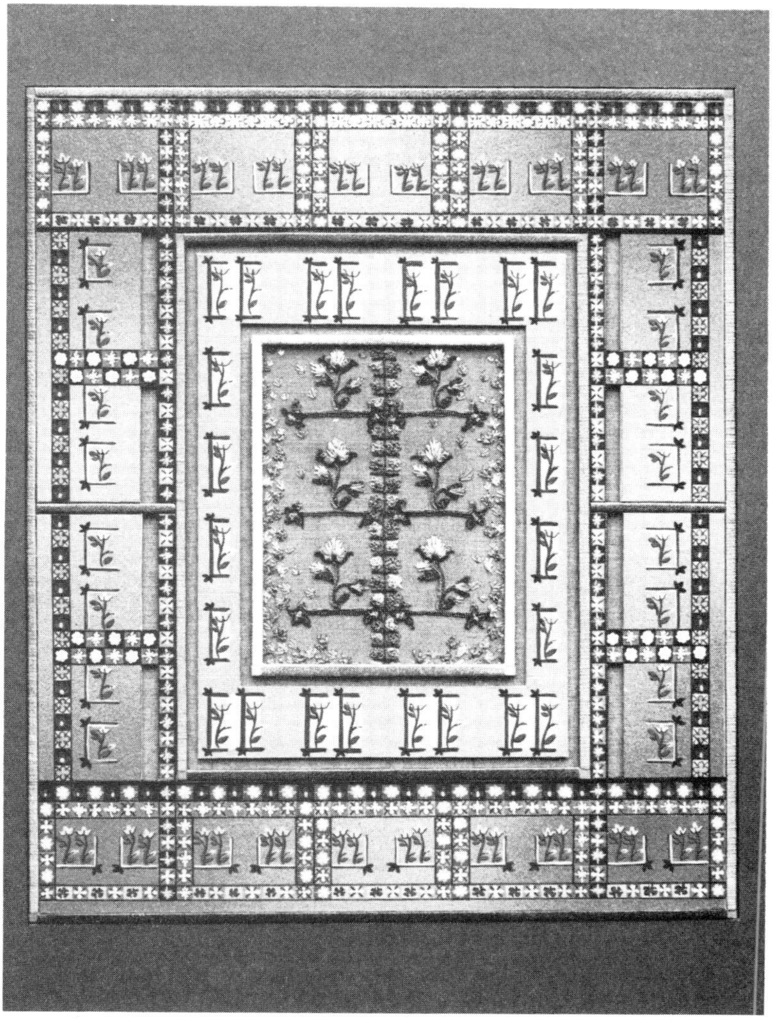

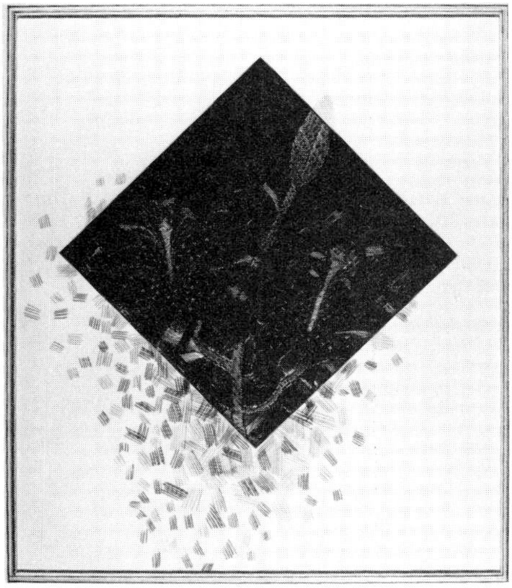

60 *'Tiger Lilies', by Isabel Dibden, in machine and hand embroidery, using cotton and rayon threads (floss) on wool challis. Crayon is used on the card mount.*

DESIGN AND MATERIALS

The principles of design we have discussed have been related to flat, two-dimensional images, but as embroiderers or fabric artists, texture is intrinsic in our work, and so design and texture should work in harmony. Often only texture is considered by the embroiderer, to the detriment of the design; the following exercises show how design and texture can be used together.

Work all these exercises on a quarter imperial-sized cartridge paper. This will not be so daunting an area to cover, but should give you enough space without cramping your design.

The following exercise shows how to build up simple shapes consisting of dots and spots. Some artists who used this dot type of technique include: *Aubrey Beardsley* (1872–98), an illustrator whose stylized drawings showed the use of dotted lines against solid areas; *Georges Seurat* (1859–91), who painted points or dots to build up areas of colour, and *Jackson Pollock* (1912–56), an exponent of action painting, who used a basis of splashes and blobs.

The dots are used to represent texture and this texture is applied to the design by sticking small, round objects to the paper. These objects can consist of small sweets, capsules, buttons, milk bottle tops, tiny rolled-up balls of paper, beads, sequins, dried pasta, rice, currants etc.

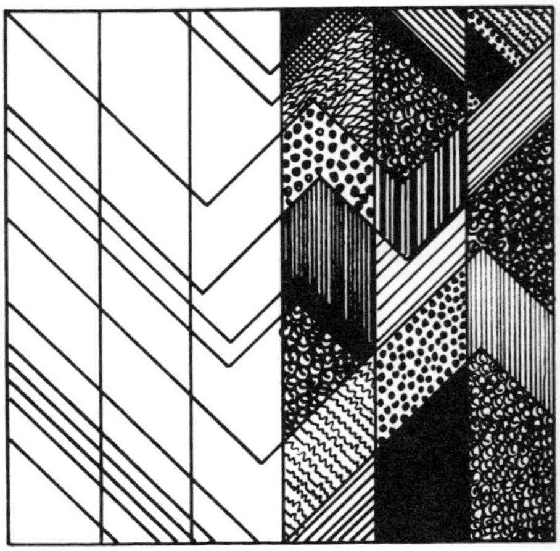

61 *Texture with geometric shape.*

Exercise 7

Draw on your paper a series of evenly spaced vertical stripes and then across these stripes mark in horizontal or zigzag bands. These bands can be of different thicknesses but they must bisect the verticals. Using your collection of small objects, decorate the entire surface of the design *(61)*. You must ensure that this decoration is not haphazard.

The initial patterns of vertical stripes and zigzags, although covered with texture, must not have their form obliterated. You should still be able to recognize the earlier drawn pattern.

The different types of texture you use must blend together, so that the design is balanced. This means that you must consider the shapes before filling them in, so that each shape remains a separate form, but when viewed in total, each shape is combined with the others to form a single design.

Exercise 8

Draw a large, simple organic shape on the paper and then fold the paper in half, then in half again, until you have four equal quarters. The design you have drawn should fit into part of each of the four segments, although one segment may contain a greater proportion of the design than the others. The design must be linked in each segment by *one* colour and *one* of the textures. So, for instance, if you are using rice as one of your textures, then the rice must be used at least once in each of the four quarters.

Fill in the shapes made in each quarter. You can keep them large and simple, or you can break down the shapes in areas of pattern. However you decide to decorate the areas, the finished design must not look disjointed; the different surface areas must blend together to form a total design *(62)*.

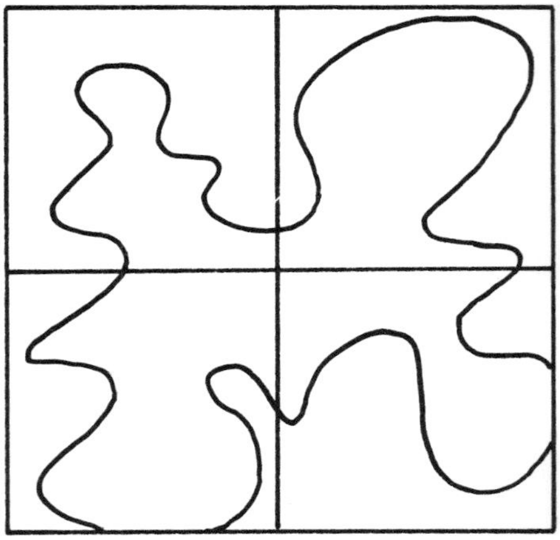

62 *Texture with organic shape.*

Exercise 9 — texture in movement

For this exercise you will need a piece of cork or pin-board for your base. Use nails, pins and drawing pins (thumb tacks) of different sizes and lengths, to build up a design of linear movement *(63)*. These lines should give the illusion of movement across the paper; they should be fluid and consist of both thick and thin lines. Adjust the heights and sizes of the pins that you use, so that the sensation of movement not only works sideways but also gives a sense of three-dimensional motion. This exercise demonstrates how the illusion of movement can be formed by the combination of line, height and proportion.

Exercise 10 — movement using relief

You can also demonstrate movement in relief by using strips of fabric, paper, ribbons etc., but for this exercise, restrict your material to paper. Cut or tear the paper into strips of various widths, and then fold or manipulate it into angles, curves and pinnacles, in a concertina-like shape. Then stick it to the background, attaching it only along the base of the structure to form a relief. Patterns can be made by grouping these relief shapes together. A textured surface has been created to give light and shade, depth and relief, while still ensuring that the design element remains strong and pleasing to the eye *(64)*.

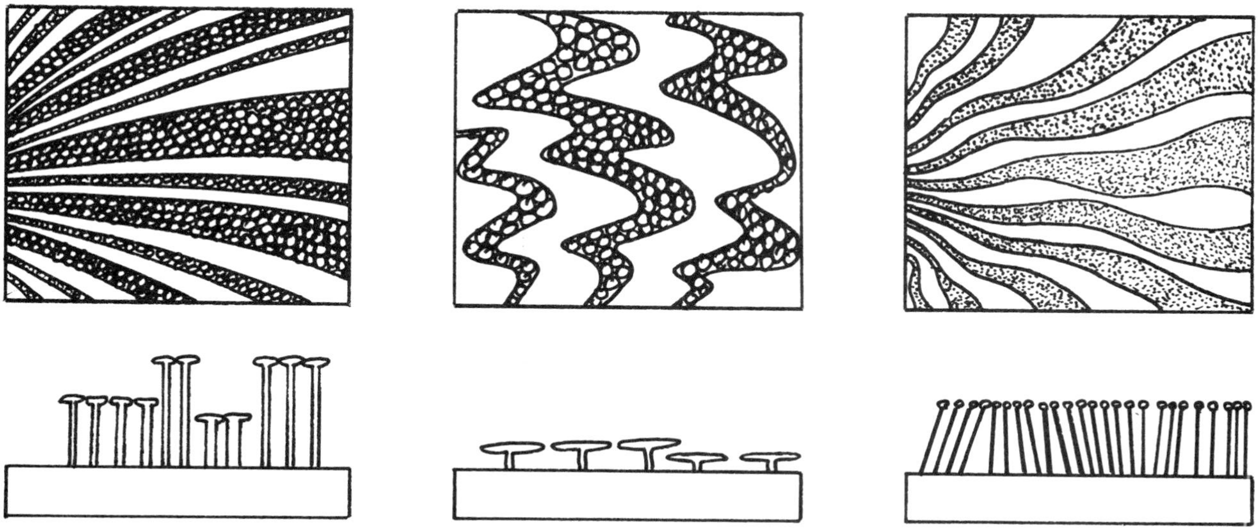

63 *Texture in movement.*

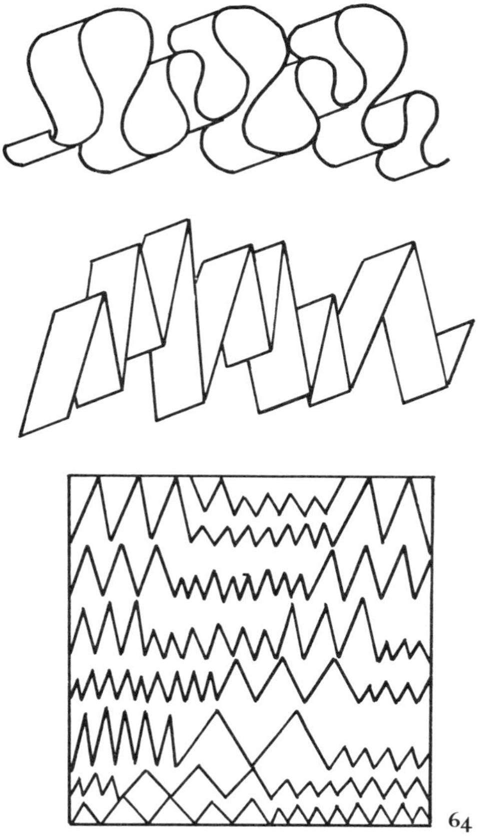

64

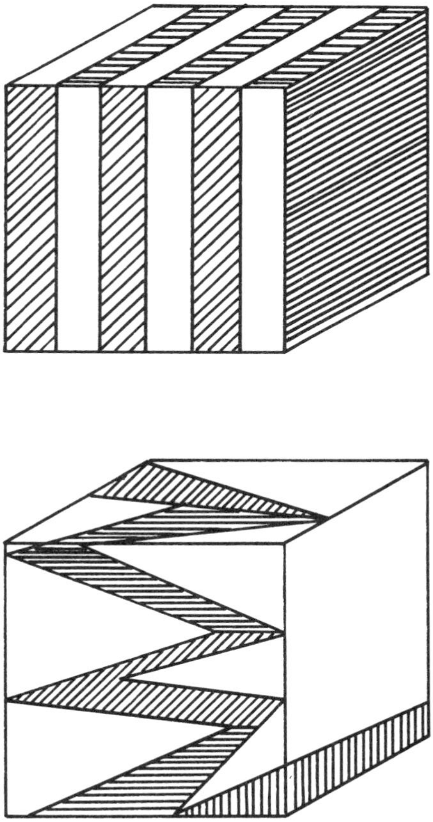

65

Exercise 11 – using texture to emphasize a shape

On your paper, draw a box shape, so that three of its sides are visible. Use lines of texture to emphasize the shape of the box. These lines can take the form of squares, geometric shapes or simple lines. The pattern used on each of the three surfaces should be different, either in scale or colour, so that the finished object should look like a three-dimensional box *(65)*.

64 *Paper relief.*

65 *Using textures to emphasize a shape.*

Exercise 12 – texture used to diminish or obliterate a shape
Draw a box of the same size as in the previous exercise; but this time, the object is to obliterate its initial shape. The lines and forms used can be organic or geometric but they must change its shape. Do not restrict the lines to each face of the object, but allow them to move over all three surfaces. Decorate these surfaces until the three-dimensional object becomes a flat, two-dimensional shape.

You can experiment further with textured surfaces by taking squares of fabric, such as velvet, corduroy, strawcloth, hessian, cotton, PVC, organza, net or silk. Try to change the nature of the fabrics by cutting, pleating, folding, sticking, burning or ironing. For instance, if velvet is cut into strips, then restuck together with the pile of the fabric lying in opposite directions, interesting effects of light and shade are produced. The pile can also be cut or burnt away to give areas of raised and flat surfaces, while the raised linear pile on corduroy can be shaved away to give sections of texture and pattern which can complement the flat surfaces.

These types of effects could be used in embroidery to suggest fields, whether grassed, newly sown or furrowed. Or the same techniques could be employed to create areas of marshland where tufts of grass or reeds are prominent on an otherwise flat surface.

Nylon fabric can be burnt by piercing the fabric with the point of a hot iron, or a still-hot extinguished match. Threads can be removed from hessian to create open and solid areas, or you can cut and pull up small areas of threads, then fray the ends to give raised tufts.

Materials such as cottons, organza or silk can be pleated and folded to create interesting shapes and give subtle tones of light and shade. For instance, if you make a tuck in a piece of cotton or silk, the light will reflect along the edge of the fold, shadowing the fabric beneath and to the side; with a transparent fabric such as organza, the folded sections will make distinctly darker lines, which can be developed into patterns. If the folding is used vertically, fences, palings or tree trunks could be suggested; if used horizontally, they could suggest the shadows found on a lake or sea.

You could further extend your design in materials by investigating the uses of thread without stitchery. These could encompass knitting, plaiting, cording, unravelling, tying, etc. See how many different experimental ways you can find to create different types of line.

Exercise 13
Using paint of one colour only, make a series of different linear marks, then try to interpret these marks in thread using the suggested techniques. Also try to show the comparisons between different types of marks – thick and thin, dull and shiny, smooth and uneven. Use ribbons, string, wool, plastic, beads, torn strips of fabric or any material which expresses the quality of the painted mark.

All of these exercises demonstrate how it is possible to blend together surface texture and design. If a little thought is given to the process, the surface of an embroidery can emphasize good design points and add more meaning to your work.

66 *'Oxfordshire Triptych', machine and hand embroidery by Kate Wells. The embroidery aims to convey a sense of wide, open spaces, but also to allow the eye to see fine details of texture.*

67 *Different shapes found within a stone wall.*

68 *A wall partly covered by ivy gives contrasting textures and shapes.*

69 *Shapes and textures found among pebbles.*

70 *Shapes and structures among stones and rocks.*

DESIGN IN LANDSCAPE

The variety of scenic beauty is unlimited – commons and pastures, lakes, rivers and mountains, coastlines and moorlands. However beautiful these scenes are, not every subject within the landscape is harmonious in its setting; but this problem can be overcome. We can take beautiful scenes and create environments of harmony, further enhancing perfection whilst retaining atmosphere.

I walk in an area of outstanding beauty, but even here, telegraph poles lurch their way up the hillside, slicing through the fields. As I am familiar with the scene, I am usually unaware of these intrusions; I have removed them from my mind's eye. As my eye has dismissed these structures, so in my drawing I must remove them from the scene, as they would not be in harmony with the atmosphere I wished to create.

In our work we seek to capture atmosphere, that is, the feeling conveyed to us by our environment. We must endeavour to retain our initial delight in a scene, however much that view is changed. We are not necessarily trying to achieve photographic accuracy.

Shapes in nature Landscape is built up of shape: superimposed shape, juxtaposed shape, organic or geometric shape. Think in terms of a jigsaw puzzle, where each piece can either be isolated or put together with others to form a composite picture.

For example, a stone wall seen from a distance will be viewed as a large, overall shape. Upon closer inspection, the construction of the form is seen to be broken down into angles, curves, rectangles, squares, wedges and other assorted shapes, usually irregular and asymmetrical *(67)*.

Many of the stones look misshapen, some have rounded edges, while others are sharply defined. There are large corner stones and rounded top stones, gaps and holes where stones are missing, crevices where wild plants grow, mosses and lichens creating other shapes and textures on its surface *(68)*. It may be a dry-stone wall where corner pieces have been cemented into place, strengthening its construction. One wall alone contains masses of information and subject matter for designs; but how often do we really look?

It would be an interesting exercise to keep a small sketchbook with you and use it to record as many different examples of shape as you can find. Begin simply, with stones and pebbles. Take one stone and draw its different facets – the outline, the structure of the stone, the shapes that make up one side; then another. Draw the shapes of the texture on the stone, the whirls and the lines and the patterns. Then put the stones together in small groups and draw these group shapes. Ask yourself the following questions as you are drawing:

1 Is there a balance between the smaller and larger stones?

2 Does one stone dominate the group?

3 Is there a difference between the textural surfaces?

4 Is there a colour change amongst the stones?

71 *Shapes found between the branches of a tree.*

5 Are new shapes being formed by the negative areas of space between the stones?

6 Are these voids darker or lighter than the stones?

Question your decisions and write your comments beside the drawings. Now look at stones collectively. Draw them on paths in gardens and woods, in heaps of rubble, in river beds and estuaries and, of course, on beaches. Ask yourself the same questions, until you become aware that you are instinctively analysing shape and carrying through the process of conscious decision-making.

Study other shapes, such as those found between the branches of trees *(71)*. Again begin by looking at one tree. Look at the spaces between the branches, then at the spaces between the leaves. Does the light change the colour of the leaves, and in doing so, does it intensify some shapes whilst modifying others? Be aware of the different leaf formations found on one tree. Consider how some leaves are overlapped while others are seen in their entirety *(72)*. When massed together they give subtle changes of light and shade, and in the process, build new structures of form and shape.

When you have looked at all these different aspects of one tree, observe a group of trees *(73)*. Take note of the spaces in between the trunks, see if the widths of the spaces are different. Look at the trunks also and note down the differences in thickness. Are they squat, chunky trunks or tall, slender ones, or is there a mixture of shapes? Do some stand behind others, and if so, do they give the illusion of looking thinner? You may notice that the trunks also change colour and those further away from you will appear 'greyer' in tone, losing their colour, while colours in the foreground will look brighter and stronger in density.

72 *Massed leaf formations show contrasting changes of light and shade. Overlapping shapes create new areas of pattern.*

73

74

75

73 *The variations and differences found in a group of trees.*

74 *Patterns and shapes between tree trunks.*

75 *Differences in tree shapes.*

If you observe again these shapes in between the trunks, you may see other, smaller forms *(75)*. You may see a hill line, bisecting the background and showing different small facets of colour and geometric shape. Looking through the tree trunks, the colour behind the trees can appear brighter than in the rest of the landscape. This is because the hard outlines of the tree trunks intensify the colours lying adjacent to them. Using the same method of observation, you can study larger groups of trees, in woods and forests. The illusion of recession can be captured by narrowing the trunks as they regress, again being very aware of the negative shapes made by the trees. Remember to keep the balance and do not have all your shapes and lines of the same proportions or thickness.

If the sun is casting shadows through the branches, draw the shapes of the shadows on the ground *(77)*. Note the angles at which they fall; are they dappled with sunlight or dark and solid, elongated or squat? Draw only the shadows, not the trees, and then try to create some simple patterns from the shapes they make.

Look at tree trunks reflected in water, in woodland pools or streams. The shapes made in the water are different from those made on land *(79)*. The shapes of the trees on the river bank are solid, while the reflected shapes are broken and diffused, being darker and stronger nearer the object reflected (i.e. by the river bank). Further away from the tree and the water's edge, the resemblance to the natural object becomes more tenuous as the reflection is dispersed.

Pattern and shape can also be seen on the bark of trees *(80)*. This is of a more

76 *A study of tree trunks by John Constable.* (Victoria and Albert Museum.)

77 *Shadows.*

78 *The sun casting elongated shadows through the trees.*

77

79 *Reflections of trees in water*. (Photo: Mike Williams.)

textural nature, but it is still worth analysing the differences between the patterns on the bark of different trees.

This textural pattern could be transposed to paper by the technique of rubbing. Take a thin piece of paper, such as detail paper, and place it over the section of bark you wish to copy. You could tape this on the edges, with masking tape, to leave your hands free and also to prevent the wind from blowing it away. Use a wax crayon gently to rub the surface of the paper, until the underneath image of the bark has been transferred to the paper.

You can use this method to collect other examples of surface texture, for example wooden walls, floors, benches, old tiles, iron gratings, rough plaster

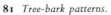

80 *The rough texture of tree bark creates unusual patterns.*

81 *Tree-bark patterns.*

82 *A working drawing showing the composition of a design.*

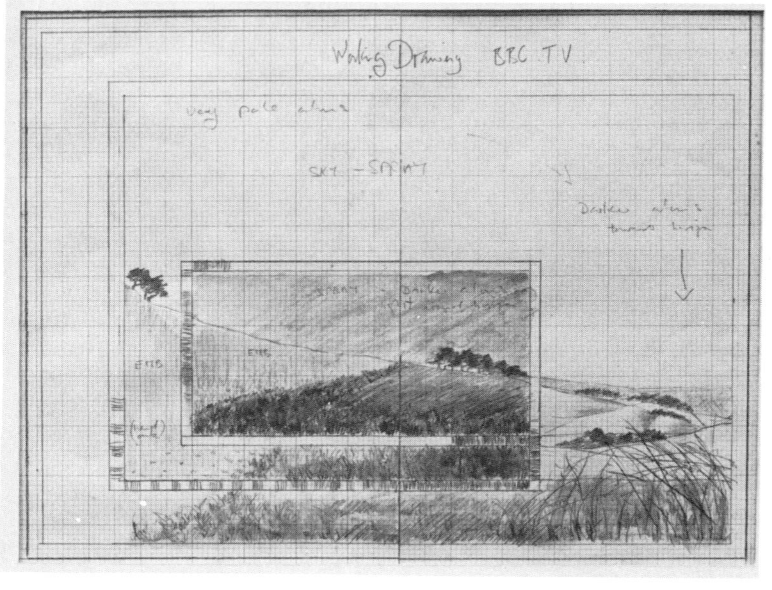

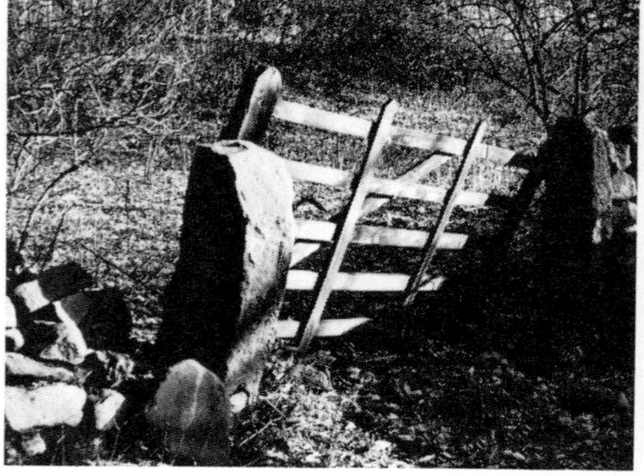

83 *The irregularity of the gateway gives added interest to this picture.*

work, shells, driftwood and any other textured surface you can find. Try to collect as many examples as possible.

Next, take a plain sheet of paper and draw out some of the patterns which have emerged from the rubbings. Draw these in line only and then, using one motif, arrange them into a pattern *(81)*. You can do this by taking a tracing from your line drawings and repeating it at regular intervals over your paper, until you have something resembling a textile print.

Take another shape and, using the same tracing process, draw out your motif on a long narrow piece of paper. Repeat the motif from the left-hand side of the paper across to the right until you have a frieze. Paint these shapes using a light and a dark colour until you have a negative and a positive image. Now retrace the whole image onto another long, thin piece of paper, but this time paint the dark shape light and the light shape dark. Compare these two images and write comments about the shapes. For instance, do the light shapes appear to recede or advance, do they appear larger or smaller than the dark shapes? Use your own powers of judgement.

These simple exercises are to enable you to practice the art of observation.

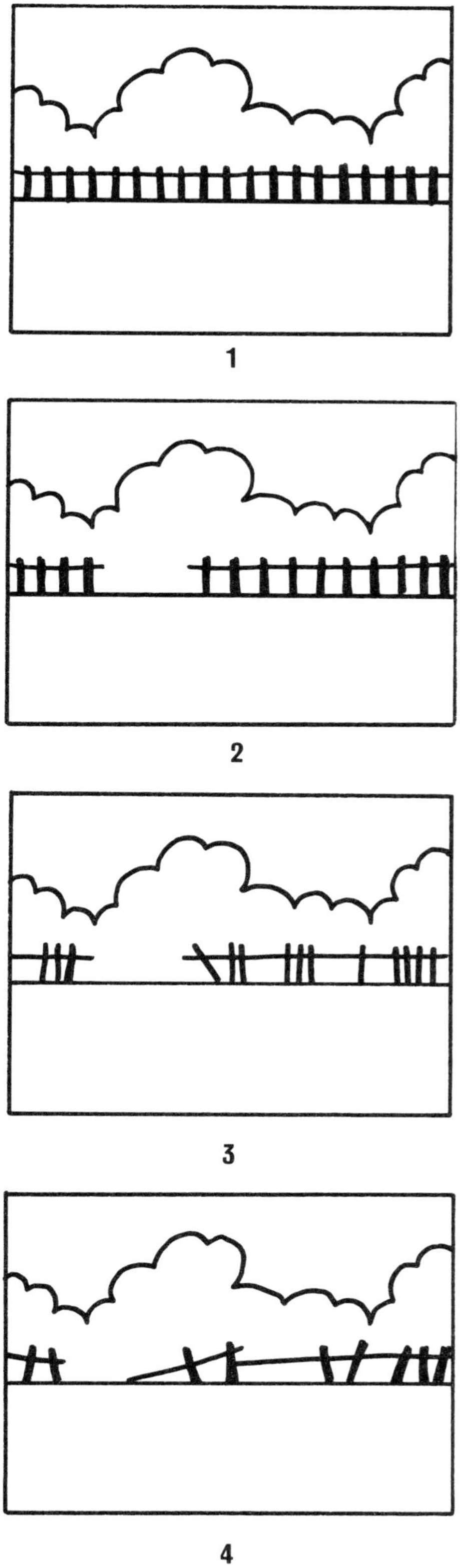

84 *Using fences to create interest.*

Composition is the technique of arranging your picture into a visible aspect of shape and mass. This aspect can be representational or abstract but whatever the composition, the arrangement of the images is critical, as bad planning will ruin good technique.

Although we are not considering embroidery at this stage, I would like to comment on the fact that I have often seen good, technical work spoilt by the maker's inability to 'see' the visual aspect of his or her work. If only embroiderers would consider the composition of the piece, before commencing the embroidery, how much better that work would be. How much better that the fruits of all that hard work should be a valid statement, pleasing the eye in all aspects!

We will now consider composition in a more practical way and use for this purpose a simple structure, seen in all areas of landscape: a wooden fence.

If we draw a simple, well-made fence, regular and solid, we will have something like that illustrated in *fig. 84.1*. So, what does it show? It is flat, static and totally uninteresting. It would be much better if we could find a fence that was a little more irregular, as in *fig. 84.2*. This fence creates interest because it is broken. It relieves the monotony of an unbroken line, and gives interest to the picture because the eye moves towards the broken section and looks through to the trees in the background, so the picture has more depth.

If we then use the same principle which we considered in the paragraphs on shape and structure (page 52) we can arrange the structure of the fence to make it visually more interesting, thereby giving the composition more vitality and movement.

In *figs 84.3* and *84.4* the shapes of the fence have been slightly changed. More palings have been added and the distance between each upright has been considered, so that each negative shape enclosed by the linear structure (i.e. the fence) is different in its proportion to that of the adjacent shape. This results in a stronger design image.

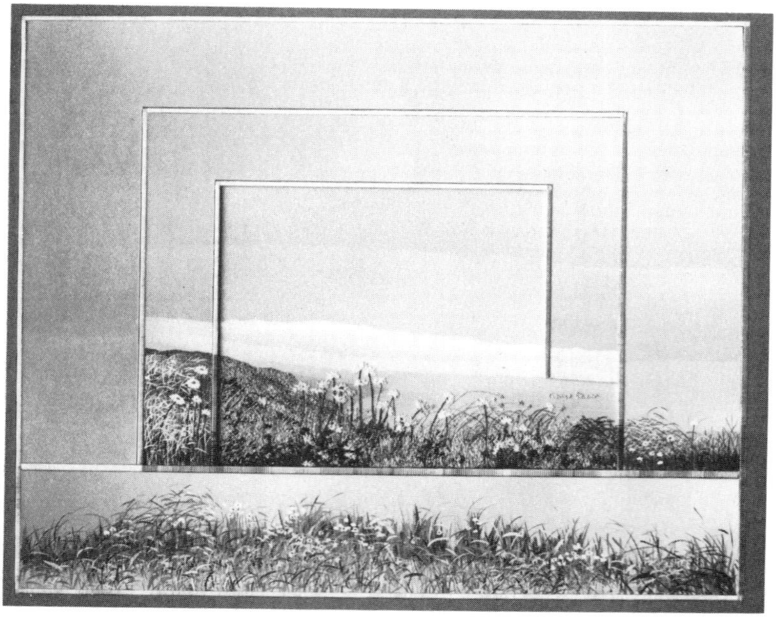

85 *A seascape showing the balance between areas of 'mass' and open spaces.*

86 *The placing of 'mass'.*

SUMMARY

1 Be discriminating in your choice of subject matter; find an area of interest within the landscape, one that has natural design potential.

2 Sketch out, in simple linear strokes, the motif, as seen in its environment; be as accurate as possible.

3 Analyse its proportions, and if necessary, extend or alternate the shapes and lines, until the object still retains the suggestion of its original form, that is, ostensibly, it is still a fence, but its basic pattern has been changed to accommodate the new design.

MASS

In landscape, mass plays an important part in the composition of the design. It must be balanced against the negative areas, here represented by the open spaces, such as low levels of water or expanses of grassland and meadows, or places where the vegetation is sparse. Tree forms obviously create mass, but so also do mountains and islands, or heavy expanses of vegetation, and this balance between the negative and positive elements in landscape is one we must seek to capture, when designing from nature.

In the first illustration in *fig. 86* there are negative areas of the landscape, the open spaces, and into these the mass must be placed. In each diagram, simple tree shapes have been drawn to illustrate the placing of mass. Observe how these forms are larger the nearer they are to the foreground, creating a sense of distance; also note that none of the shapes has been placed directly in the centre of the picture.

THE HORIZON LINE

This illusion of distance can be illustrated, not only by the vertical scale of the placement of mass, but also by the positioning of the horizon line, together with the treatment of the foreground. For instance, if the horizon line is placed high, that is, above the centre of the paper, the appearance of distance can be

87 *A design showing the placement of a high horizon line to create distance.*

88 *Distance within a field.*

increased by some simple methods, illustrated in *fig. 88*.

For the *far distance*, keep the lines horizontal and closely spaced near the eye level.

For the *middle distance*, open up the horizontal lines and put in some low diagonals, adding areas of texture amongst the grasses.

For the *foreground*, the lines can be verticals and sharp diagonals, representing foreground grasses. Detail can be put in with flowers and foliage. Do not, however, allow the foreground detail to reach above the horizon line as this will destroy the illusion of distance.

The *illusion of nearness* can be achieved by making the foreground more relevant. In *fig. 90*, the horizon line is placed below the centre of the paper and the foreground detail is allowed to break the eye level, thus giving importance to the front of the design.

1 Place the horizon line below centre.

2 The positioning of an area of mass, such as a large tree, in the middle distance, gives a impression of solidity and depth, but remember not to place it mid-centre.

3 The foreground details are of prime importance: they reach into the sky, break the eye level and give the sense of 'looking through' the grasses into the landscape beyond.

89 *In this design the greater proportion of detail has been kept below the horizon line.*

90 *Creating foreground interest.*

92 *Contrast within a landscape.*

93 *A sharp contrast between dark mountains and a sunlit foreground.* (Photo: Mike Williams.)

91 *The centre of interest is in front of the lake.*

93

THE FOCAL POINT

The focal point is the centre of interest, around which you will build your picture. If you find an element of landscape that appeals to you, such as a rugged cliff, a lake or an estuary, you can then use that as your main element – it is your theme. You may wish to add other forms to your focal point, or to take out shapes which do not appeal to you.

For example, the embroidery illustrated in *fig. 91* uses the lake as the focal point, the centrepiece of the work. The horizon line is above centre, with the hills rising above it to give the illusion of distance. The front section of the hills is embroidered to suggest tree forms, which brings this part of the embroidery forward. The embroidered grasses in the immediate foreground give interest to that area and also break the plain expanse of fabric representing water. So, in this picture, I have selected my focal point, balanced the mass with the void, given the composition depth and finally added interest by the use of detail.

You may decide that your focal point is not necessarily an object, but perhaps an area of contrast within a landscape. It may be brooding, dark mountains above a sunlit meadow, dark trees against the snow, or a mass of flowers beside bare rocks. The focal point may not be so obvious as any of these, so you will have to strengthen one area or find the most interesting shapes and create a centre of interest.

For example, make the brooding mountains larger and stronger, so that they dominate the picture (93); doing this makes the sunlit meadow appear brighter, and balanced against the darkness of the background.

If you are drawing rocks on a beach, do not attempt to draw in every rock, and do not space them out equally. Group them together, making one rock larger than the others, balancing the massed areas against the open spaces of the beach. You may be particularly interested in the sky and its cloud formation, and wish this to be the focal point, dominating the picture. So the proportion of sky should be greater than the area of land, as this will immediately give the sky greater importance. The shapes of the clouds need to be considered and perhaps rearranged. If there are a lot of little clouds, it would be better to fuse them together to form some larger masses or the whole area could be in danger of becoming bitty (compare the two diagrams in *fig. 94*).

I have repeatedly used the horizon line as a means for dividing the picture and obtaining illusions of depth, recession or prominence, but we have only discussed the use of one horizon line.

It is possible, however, to use different horizon levels and viewpoints within the same design. For example, you can show, in the same picture, a field seen from a distance and from close up. You can view the distant horizon and also see other viewing parameters. For example, in the winter landscape in *colour plate 1*, the hill line takes the eye to the distant horizon, but the flowers and grasses of the foreground against the open sprayed sky strengthen the illusion of standing on the edge of a hill overlooking the valley. The painted section of the bottom strip brings the immediate foreground into focus and strengthens the frontal section.

94

95 *Cloud formations give interest to sky areas.*

96a *Design sheet based on an Italian garden, showing three viewpoints.*

In the Italian garden design *(96a)*, there are three main viewpoints. The eye is directed initially to the central inner landscape, which gives depth to the main area of the design, but the introduction of two other viewpoints jolts the consciousness into an awareness of other events taking place in the picture plane. Although the whole piece evokes an air of peace and tranquillity, the different viewpoints create the illusion of looking through and beyond the immediate image of the textured garden, thereby adding an element of fantasy to the design.

We have considered shape and composition in some detail and before applying this to embroidery, it would be beneficial at this stage to carry out a simple design.

96b *Design sheet showing patterned borders.*

97

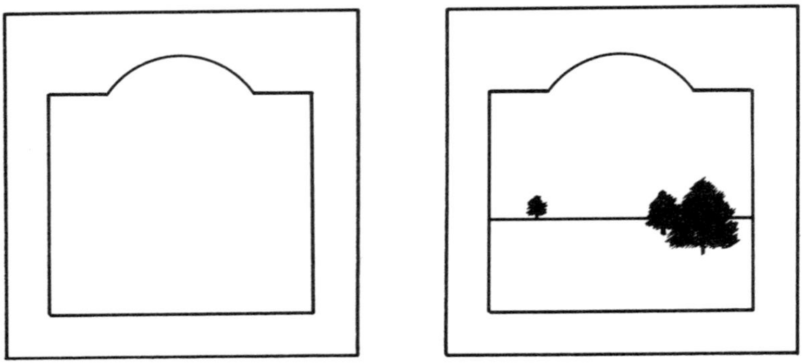

98

99

100

Exercise 14

1 Using graph paper, draw a square of approximately 15 cm (6 in.).

2 Take one of the shapes shown in *fig.* 97 and put it into the square.

3 Now add one horizon line and three tree shapes *(98)*.

4 Decorate the outside border with simple motifs of flowers or foliage and add other lines if this will help the composition.

I have added another horizon line to the picture *(99)*. This has broken up the field area and given the centre tree an anchor. I have also added a border to the central shape and the outside square, and filled in the remaining space with a trellis pattern. To connect the central trees with the border, I have put in a stylized tree shape and repeated this in the inner border.

In the final design, detail has been added within the trellis work to give texture and colour *(100)*.

3 Colour

Before you begin using colour in embroidery, it is a good idea to understand some of the principles of colour, and in order to do this, you should carry out the following exercises. These are designed to take you easily through some of the theories of colour.

At the core of all colour experiments are the basic colours, known as the primaries.

PRIMARY COLOURS

Red
Yellow
Blue

If we take two of these primary colours and mix them together, we create what is known as a secondary colour. So, for instance, mixing together red and yellow gives orange.

SECONDARY COLOURS

Red + yellow = orange
Yellow + blue = green
Red + blue = purple

The next stage is to mix together a primary colour with a secondary colour; so, basically, you are using a mixture of three colours to create a new single colour.

TERTIARY COLOURS

Blue + green = blue-green
Red + green = brown
Yellow + green = yellow-green

From the three primary pigments of pure colour, you can create a variety of other colours by mixing the paints together in three simple stages – primary, secondary, and tertiary, mixes of one, two and three colours.

EXERCISES USING PAINT

Exercise 1 – primary colours
To mix up a colour chart you need a sheet of white cartridge paper, a soft-bristled brush (no. 2 or 3) and either gouache or acrylic paints. From the paints, choose the three primaries of red, yellow and blue and find what is known as the middle tone. A middle tone simply means that it is a pure colour and does not contain tints of other colours. For example, a middle yellow would not contain either more blue, to make it a greenish-yellow, nor would it contain more red, to make it an orange-yellow; it would be a pure, clear yellow.

Paint a 2.5 cm (1 in.) square of middle red, middle yellow and middle blue, at the top of your paper. Leave spaces of approximately 10 cm (4 in.) in between each colour.

101 *Three primary colours.*

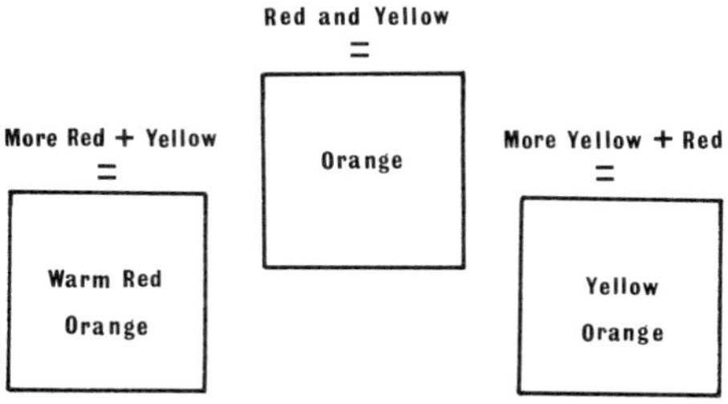

102 *Variations on secondary tones.*

Exercise 2 — secondary colours

Mix equal quantities of red and yellow together until you have orange, and paint another small square underneath the top red square.

Mix more red to the yellow, so that the proportion of red paint is greater than yellow. You should have a warm reddish-orange. Paint this coloured square to the left of the orange square.

Finally, add a greater proportion of yellow to the red primary, until you have a cool yellow-orange. Paint this square to the right of the orange square.

Using the same process, mix the yellow and blue together to give greens:

Equal amounts of yellow + blue = green
More yellow + less blue = yellow-green
More blue + less yellow = blue-green

Finally mix together the red and the blue to give purple:

Red + blue = purple
More red + blue = red-purple
More blue + red = blue-purple

After these exercises you should have secondary colours.

Exercise 3 — tertiary colours

Now you can mix up some examples of tertiary colours. To begin with, mix the blue primary colour with the secondary green, so:

Blue + green = blue-green
Blue + orange = ochre-brown
Blue + purple = rich purple-blue

Repeat this process and mix the yellow primary colour with a secondary colour.

Yellow + green = yellow-green (leaf green)
Yellow + orange = light yellow-orange
Yellow + purple = warm brown

Finally, repeat with the red primary:

Red + green = red-brown
Red + orange = rich, warm, dark orange
Red + purple = rich purple-brown

103

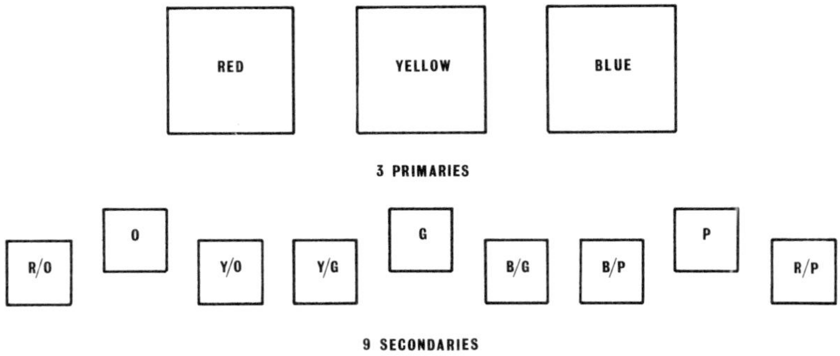

You have now built up a range of colours from the pure primaries through many different hues. You may think that some of the tertiary colours look sludgy and consider rejecting these tones. However, before you dismiss the browns and greys, think of how they can work to complement other shades. For example, in nature, the browns work with the green tones in a landscape – browns might emphasize the green foliage of a tree. Likewise, for using primaries and secondaries together, look at how the yellow of a gorse bush stands out on a green hillside. Put that gorse bush on a hill covered with bracken and you have yellow, green and brown – primary, secondary and tertiary colours – harmonizing in the landscape.

To go back to the colour exercises, you can also add black or white to the colours you have mixed and create even more shades. The addition of black, however, needs to be carefully controlled, otherwise you will end up with a dark mess. Add the black a speck at a time until you have darkened the colour to the tone required.

Exercise 4
Try adding a little black to each of the new secondary and tertiary colours and paint them on the same sheet of white paper as the other exercises. Repeat the process, but this time use white instead of black. You may notice that, with the addition of white, the hues increase in luminosity but decrease in terms of purity and richness. Indeed, if you add too much white the colour may become chalky.

In my own painting I use very little black, preferring to tone down my bright colours with more subdued shades, and I often use tertiary colours for this purpose. For example, a bright blue can be greyed by the introduction of a little burnt umber (a shade of brown). A green, such as Hooker's green, when mixed with burnt umber, gives a lovely foliage green, which works well for shadows amongst leaves.

Reds, such as a cadmium red, when mixed with blue, give lovely dark tones which are good for shadows on mountains. Try mixing alizarin crimson, which is a bright, purplish-red, with yellow, to give lovely warm orange, like ripe peaches or golden chrysanthemums. Mix the same alizarin crimson with blue and you get the colour of African violets. As for mixing yellow, try cadmium yellow light, and mix with red to give the colour of a Jaffa orange or a summer sunset, then mix the same yellow with blue to create the colour of a pine forest edging the sea.

TONE

Tone is the gradation of colour from light to dark. One colour can have many tones, ranging in brightness from dark shades through to light. Look at a paint chart or a colour chart of threads and you will see the various changes in tone of one colour.

For instance, take a blue and paint it onto a piece of paper without using water, so that it is thick. Now try to lighten and darken that colour, adding black or white (mixed with water) and see how many different shades you can achieve from the one colour.

You can also have two different colours which are the same tone. These two

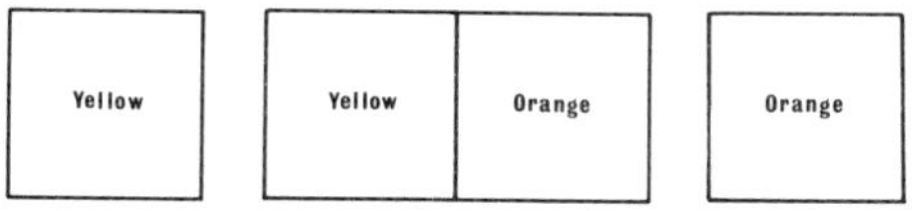

104 *Simultaneous contrast.*

colours have the same quality of brightness, the same depth of colour. In the previous chapter on design I used the blacks and whites on a television screen to illustrate this particular point. If you look, for instance, at two autumn trees, one may be a bright orange-brown, the other perhaps a bright russet. They are different in colour but because they both have the same degree of brightness and intensity, they can be said to be of the same *tone*. The pale, fading yellow-green leaves of an adjacent tree are not only of a different colour, but also of a different tone.

You can also achieve a simultaneous contrast by placing two tones side by side so that they react together. For example, put a square of Naples yellow beside a square of lemon yellow; the Naples yellow looks browner and the lemon yellow takes on a tinge of green. Each colour is reacting simultaneously with its neighbour; pull the colours apart and they revert to their original shade.

Exercise 5

Try painting a square of yellow on the left-hand side of the piece of paper, and a square of orange on the right side. In the middle paint a square of yellow, adjacent to the orange. You can now see that the orange square takes the warmth from the juxtaposed yellow, while the yellow square, in losing its warmth, looks greener and therefore cooler. The adjacent colours have reacted to each other simultaneously, while the outside colours have retained their own character.

This effect happens many times in my own work. I may choose two separate reels of colour, but after machining them, find that they visually interreact and change from their original hues. So, even after many years of using colour, I am still sometimes taken unawares; but this, to me, is the fascination of colour.

If you look at the simple colour circle *(105)*, you will see that opposite the three primaries are the secondary colours – orange, green and purple. These colours are said to be complementary, which means that the primary colours contrast with the secondary colours; so orange is complementary to blue, green is complementary to red, and purple is complementary to yellow; they contrast with each other.

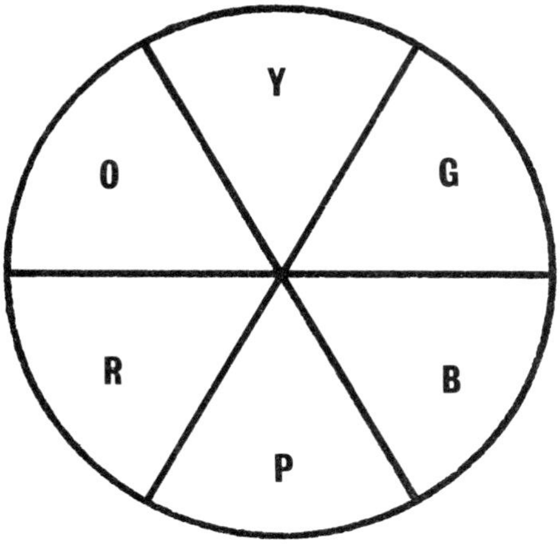

105 *The colour circle.*

Exercise 6

Using two colours, red and green, paint three squares of green on a piece of paper; into the first square, paint another smaller square of the red complementary colour. In the second square, paint a larger square of red, and in square three, paint only a dot of red *(106)*.

Now look closely at each square. You will see that in the first square, the red

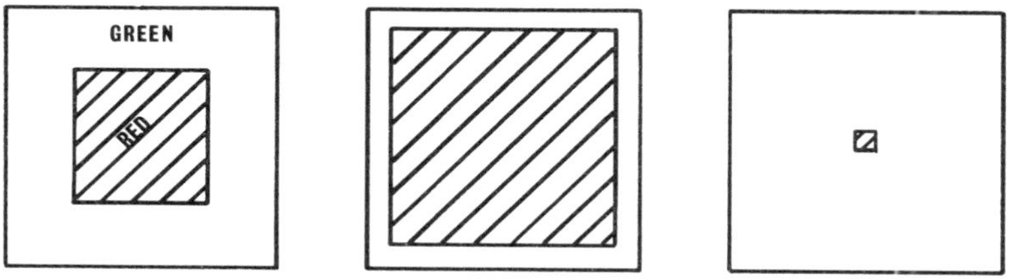

106 *Complementary colours.*

appears to vibrate against the green. In square two, the larger red square appears to be higher than the green square, while in the third square the red dot seems to diminish and recede into the background. These are all optical illusions and show how complementary colours react on each other when in different proportions.

Exercise 7
Another interesting experiment you may like to try, using red and green, is to take the two colours and by varying the degree of saturation of one colour by another, move from red to green.

Paint a square of middle red on the left side of the paper, and add a small quantity of green to the paint. Each time you mix a little more green, lessen the amount of red and paint a square on your paper. Carry on doing this until you finally have all green and no red *(107)*. This exercise illustrates how much colour can be absorbed by another; it shows the colour's quality of saturation.

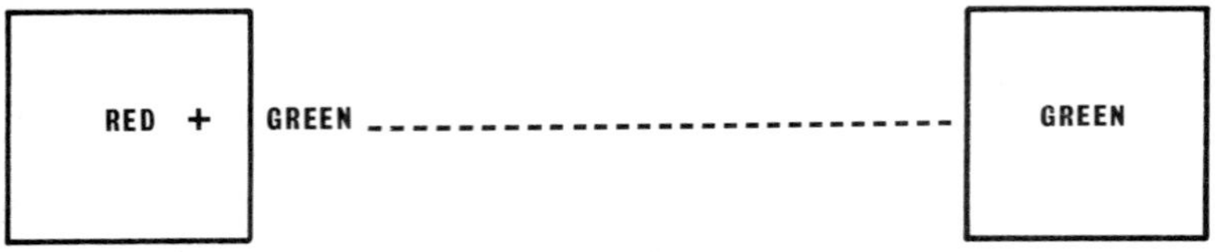

107 *Varying the degree of colour saturation.*

Exercise 8
When we consider using threads in embroidery we shall be looking at how one colour changes another when put next to it. To illustrate this point, again using paint, find a middle grey, one that is neither too cool nor too warm. For instance, if you look at a grey sky, you may see yellows or blues in the grey, but you want a grey in which these other hues are not apparent.

Paint three squares, one each of red, yellow and blue. Into the centre of each of the primary coloured squares, add a small square of grey *(108)*. Then look for any colour reaction. In square one the grey against the red will look blue. In square two the grey on the yellow will look greenish, while in square three the grey on the blue will seem to lose its colour and will look cooler. So even neutral greys can change their appearance when put next to the colour, and these reactions will happen in your embroidery; it is important to be aware that colours react with each other and change their appearance.

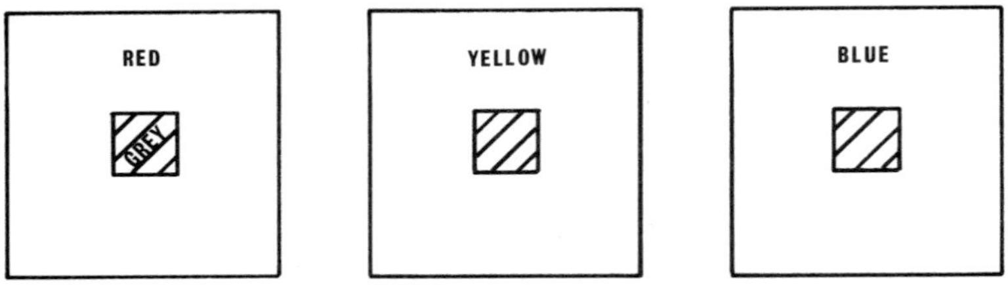

108 *Colour reaction.*

1 *Enchantment touches moonlight's pale tones.* The contrast between the dark clouds, airbrushed on silk and the sunlight on distant woods, hand painted in silk dyes, draws the eye into the design. The foreground detail of wild flowers in whip stitch and tall grasses in long and short stitch is completed by a painted band in acrylics.

2 *Threads of changing colour, reflecting nature's seasons.* The distant hills, dotted with woods and trees, hand painted in silk dyes, flow across the picture in a single season, while in the foreground winter, spring, summer and autumn change in a continuous blend of colour and shape using machine embroidered whip stitch and acrylics on card.

3 (opposite) *In English lanes green the summer foxglove grows.* The massed textures and shades of green found in a bank of nettles contrast with a single cerise foxglove, all completed in machine embroidered whip stitch. A thin bound border in silk threads separates the overhanging trees, in whip stitch, from a summer sky, in airbrushed acrylics.

4 (opposite) *Gifts of the earth.* In whip stitch on a sprayed silk background, the central section shows a rich profusion of flowers gathered around a lush woodland lakeside which is extended in a card border painted in acrylics.

5 *In the estuary's shallow water, sea grasses grow.* A high horizon line, airbrushed in silk dyes, gives extra emphasis to sea and beach, while sea grasses are completed in whip stitch. To provide a contrast, the outer border, in acrylics on card, reverses this proportion, using a greater expanse of sky.

6 *Beyond a magical garden the secret valley lies.* Flowers and illusionary trees in whip stitch on a sprayed silk background are used to create a mysterious landscape. Acrylic painted card insets in the foreground lead the eye inwards to a world which is part real and part fantasy.

7 (opposite) *Purity is a lily, within a landscape white.* Using airbrushed acrylics across both silk and card, the detailed flower painting is in gouache with a combination of whip stitch and french knots as seeding.

8 *Pale grasses stand sentinel over misty valleys blue.* The central section shows an atmospheric landscape, airbrushed on silk, contrasting with the fine tracery of Queen Anne's Lace in whip stitch and wild grasses in long and short stitch. The card surround, painted in acrylics, is separated by a thin border bound in silk thread.

Try experimenting with colour for yourself, so that you build up an intuitive knowledge of colour, which will help you when you come to plan out colour schemes. You will also be more aware of what the visual colour reaction will be when you want to place two different colours together.

USING COLOUR TO SUGGEST MOODS

Colour has always been used to suggest moods and feelings. Red, for example, gives a sense of excitement; too much can be overpowering but used in the right proportion it can give vitality to a work. Constable often painted a little red amongst his greens to enliven or 'lift' the painting. Blues give a sense of calm and serenity but they can also be used to suggest coolness, so work well in winter scenes. Yellows are bright, sunny colours, giving an illusion of happiness.

THE SYMBOLIC USE OF COLOUR

Besides creating moods and feelings, colours also have symbolic significance in many different areas. For example, in the design of Oriental carpets, colours play an important role, as each colour has its own meaning:

Red happiness and joy
Green spring and rebirth
Purple the king's colour
Indigo solitude

In ecclesiastical embroidery symbolism is also highly significant. Green is again used to represent spring and re-birth, the promise of fruitfulness and hope. Other examples are:

Red the colour of blood or of fire
Green hope, rebirth, the colour of Trinity
Purple royal majesty
Blue eternity, faith, truth

It is interesting to note that in these two lists of colour symbolism, which represent different cultures and creeds, the meanings of the colours have a marked similarity. In my own work I use greens to represent spring or summer, a time of rebirth and hope. Blues, from pale to dark, suggest winter in all its solitude, holding its truth of the coming spring. Golds and yellows are used in warm autumn landscapes, showing the wealth and abundance of the fruits and berries of this mellow season. Colour has always played an important role, not only in how we see it, but in how we use and interpret its symbolism.

COLOURS OF THE SEASONS

We live in a world of colour and must, therefore, reflect that world in our work. However abstract the design, we still use colour, even if the tones are darks or neutrals. How we use and balance colour gives our work its individuality. After the previous basic exercises, you will, I hope, be able to use colour more confidently.

The year is divided into seasons and each season has its own character, which can be emphasized by the use of colour.

Winter At first glance, there appears to be an absence of colour in a winter landscape, but this is deceptive, for although the tones and hues may be subdued, colour is indeed present. The greys and browns predominate, but what a wealth of shades can be found, from stone-coloured greys, blue slate-greys, leaden greys and mouse-greys through to all the browns. Brown may seem a dull colour, but think of bay and chestnut, umber, cinnamon, chocolate and tawny, khaki or russet. Immediately colour is pressed upon the senses, winter loses its initial drabness.

I witnessed an interesting colour phenomenon one winter, whereby a colour was completely changed when lightly covered in snow. Lying beneath a small copse of trees was a carpet of fallen beech leaves, and this was covered by a light scattering of snow. The sky was a heavy grey and the tree trunks looked slate-blue in the light. Instead of being russet and tawny with the beech leaves, the ground beneath the trees had turned pink. The russet and white together gave an optical illusion of soft pinks.

I continued my journey across the moorland and this same illusion was occurring where the snow had lightly fallen on brackens and dried heathers. The whole of the moorland expanse was shaded in tones of soft pinks, greys and moss greens, and all this was taking place in December, with snow falling; there *is* colour in a winter landscape.

The greens in a winter landscape will be apparent, but the tones are subdued, often with a hint of brown, olive, sage and pale moss-green, rather than the brighter emeralds of summer. Blacks and whites will predominate in a snow scene but again, look for all the different tones of black, ranging from jet and ink, to raven or sloe, while some whites can be chalky, silver or milk.

Exercise 9

To illustrate the different tones of one colour, try to collect as many different whites as possible. Cut out various types of paper and fabric, and stick them onto a sheet of paper. Make your examples approximately 2.5 cm (1 in.) square. The short list I have included is only to help start your collection; see if you can find at least another 12 examples.

Whites

tracing paper	cotton wool	watercolour
cartridge paper	cotton fabric	gouache
note paper	silk fabric	acrylic paint
kitchen towel	net	poster paint

If you feel really energetic, you can try the same exercise with blacks, then greys and browns, until you have built up a range of personalized colour charts.

Apart from the natural colours found in the countryside, the feeling of winter can be suggested by the use of cool colours. In my own work I use blues to give the impression of cold landscapes. I like to mix the shades, ranging from indigo and dark navy to sapphire and azure. The balance of colour is important: the

109 *A watercolour of flowers and grasses found in Brittany.*

darker, colder colours lend themselves to winter twilights or cold, moonlit nights, while pale azures, turquoise and ice blues suggest frost and snows. They give sparkle to the landscape without the obvious additions of glitter.

One point to remember is that cool tones give the illusion of recession, so if you want to bring the foreground forward, add some warmer shades. For example, warm browns, ochres, soft pinks or beiges, will add warmth, and contrast with the cooler background tones; they will also help to give depth to the picture.

Spring This is a time of renewal and hope, when young, fresh colour is transforming the landscape. Fresh colour is very important here, as it is the impression of young growth you are trying to capture; the colours should therefore be clear and pure. Apple-greens, lime-greens, yellow and white form a sound basic colour scheme. Into this background you can add splashes of colour – pink cherry-blossom, hawthorn, snowdrops, yellow daffodils, tulips and crocus.

Gardens and parks would obviously give brighter patches of colour, but the landscape in the early spring has more subtle tones. Look for the sallow-greys of the catkins, the browns and greens of the buds about to burst forth, soft rain-washed skies, or the early sunlight on dew-spangled grass; also remember that spring foliage is lighter in colour and texture than the dense, heavy masses of summer.

Spring conveys a gentleness, illustrated by the soft tones of background colour, and into those delicate shades, brighter colours can be added to give light or depth.

One spring, in Sardinia, I watched the island landscape transformed from its dry browns and olive-greens into a carpet of sea-pinks with silver-green foliage; and the fields and waysides were covered in red poppies. It is interesting to note the different colours in the British landscape compared to those of other countries, so if ever you spend a holiday abroad, take along your sketchbook and box of watercolours and record those colours.

Fig. 109 shows my own record of the flowers and grasses found along the coastal region of southern Brittany in May.

Exercise 10

Try to collect as many coloured pictures as you can of scenes depicting flowers, grasses, skies, rivers etc., pictures which to you epitomize the essence of spring. Use these as references whenever you need to create spring pictures in the depths of winter. A collection such as this will refresh your memory and help you choose the correct tones and colours of spring.

Summer Green symbolizes the essence of summer: verdant, emerald, grass-green, bright with the myriad colours of flowers and foliage. The summer landscape has such an abundance of colour that it can very easily become overwhelming. When portraying a summer landscape, selection is important and often what you leave out of the picture can heighten the dramatic aspect of the season. For instance, you may want to emphasize the greenness of the landscape, but too many other colours would detract from that aim, so it would be preferable to add only one or two contrasting colours, but include many shades of green.

Colour plate 3 shows various tones of green, but the introduction of the foxglove brings the entire picture to life. If, however, I had added more buttercups or bluebells, the impact of the single contrast would have been lost.

The colours of summer are more intense and warmer than those of spring. Skies are more dramatic, and often on a sunny day the sky is bluer and darker at the top, then pale towards the horizon. The pale tones are still warm, often with touches of yellow ochre. Even on cloudy, rainy days, the sky retains a warmth in its grey, and touches of blue show where the sky appears through the clouds. Seas and lakes reflect the colour of the sky and shimmer in the clearer summer light, whilst moving water, although still reflecting the sky, is broken into a pattern of lights and shadow.

In summer months shadows are stronger; patches of dark greens, tinged with purples or browns, lie under trees and hedgerows. In some instances the shadows are so dark that they appear as black, but look again and you will see magenta, umber and indigo. You can also suggest the impression of heat by the correct use of colour. For example, to create the atmosphere of a hot, sunny day, use ochres and sienna, oranges, golds and yellow, intermingled with dark greens. A bright blue sky, reflected in the blue or cornflowers, or the occasional splash of a red poppy, all help to conjure up the atmosphere of a hot day.

Exercise 11

Using coloured rectangular shapes of cut-out paper, make an abstract pattern, depicting a hot, sunny day. The design can be as small or as large as you wish, but try to balance the colours, so that the final impression is one of heat and sunshine.

Repeat the same exercise, only this time use shapes of as many different types of green, introducing one bright colour. You are aiming for an effect of verdant abundance, as found deep in a summer woodland.

Autumn This is a time of nostalgia, a magical season of glorious colour – russet, chestnut, cinnamon and gold, ruby reds and purple heathers. It is a season of mists, of clear bright blue skies, black and red berries, drying grasses and falling leaves. Above all, it is the colour of autumn which lingers in the memory.

The colour can be very tonal, with many different shades of browns and rust and some sage greens. The greens of autumn are not as vivid as in a summer landscape, and the yellows not as acid as those found in the spring. The autumn colours in Britain seem to vary from year to year; sometimes reds and browns predominate, in other years the colours are golds and yellows. Depending on the weather and the time of day, autumn colours can be mellow and soft or spectacularly vivid. This vivid colour scheme is especially noticeable on the East Coast of America, in New England, where the colours are intensely beautiful.

Early mornings in autumn often bring with them pearly shades of mist, hanging suspended over valleys or shrouding trees and fields. Mist seems to rise up from the riverbeds, leaving impressions of unreality, muffling sounds and changing shapes. As the mist rises, and the sun breaks through, beautiful patterns can be observed on hedgerows, grasses and fields where tiny drops of dew reflect the sun's light, and sometimes a small miracle can be seen, when an entire field is converted into a quilt of gossamer, with tiny insect webs sparkling with the colours of the rainbow. A similar effect can be seen on those mornings of early frost, where clear bright skies contrast with the pale silvery, grey-green grasses, with all shades of browns and beiges predominating.

Fallen leaves symbolize autumn, but have you ever noticed the colour difference between the dry, curled leaves and those same leaves when wet? Look also at how one side of a leaf is a different colour to the other.

Exercise 12
Collect as many different-coloured leaves as possible and try to stick them down on paper to form a collage. Grade the tones from lights to darks, so that you move from the pale yellows and golds through to the tawnies, deep browns and reds. This exercise is to show how many different tones and colours can be found from one source, in this case, leaves.

Exercise 13
Using the petals of flowers, leaves and berries, make a collage of colour, introducing primary, secondary and tertiary colours. Note down at the top of your paper how many colours you use and try to group them under their correct colour headings.

Colour plate 2 shows a large landscape depicting all four seasons. The seasons change from winter in the outside left-hand band, to spring, summer in the central section, then autumn and finally back to winter again in the right-hand, outside band. The vista shows the same continuous landscape, but the changing seasons are suggested by the colours associated with spring, summer, autumn and winter. This interpretation could easily become disjointed and 'bitty' because of the many colours, but by blending the tones and hues together this mistake was avoided.

I achieved this by introducing one colour in different proportions into the seasonal band. For instance, the blue tones run throughout the outside winter bands, into the sky, uniting the upper sections of the design. I have also introduced the blues into the landscape by embroidering or painting blue flowers. The yellow flowers echo the tones of spring and autumn and these are also introduced into the summer section, and the winter whites are again brought into the picture by the summer daisies. The actual seasons have been separated by wrapped silk bands, lightly blending together the adjacent colours.

So, by co-ordinating the colours and keeping the same continuous landscape, I was able to integrate the four seasons without losing the composition of the design.

As well as being used to create seasonal changes, colour can also indicate atmospheric effects. Skies, for instance, are constantly changing canvases of tone and hue. From dawn to dusk the colour and light changes both the sky and the landscape, highlighting or casting shadows. Grey skies can sum up thoughts of April rain or soft autumn mists, of lashing hail and howling winds, of skies wild and thunderous, or leaden with snow; all greys, all different, but each one representing a particular element. The grey of the sea changes to blue, turquoise or navy, depending on the time of day, night or season. When the sky changes, so too does the colour of the land. Watch the changing shades of the summer sunset, the reds and golds flooding the sea, sky and land. Then compare them with winter's fading light, where the colours are cooler, suggesting ice; shades of lilac and pale turquoise hug the skyline, changing to the inky blues of the heavens.

The science of colour can be taught, but its intuitive use must come from within, and for that process to be a spontaneous reaction you must be aware of the changing nature of colour, and to be aware, you must *look*.

110 *A nineteenth-century American log-cabin patchwork quilt, worked in velvets, silks and taffeta. The colours are rich maroon, blue and burgundy in velvets, fading to pale pinks, blues and natural colours in silks.*

111 *'Papaver', a quilt by Isabel Dibden showing machine quilting and machine embroidery. A variety of fabrics was employed: silks, lawn, cotton, satins, wools and voiles. The flowers featured relate to the colours of the triangles of cloth on which they are embroidered.*

COLOUR AND TEXTILES

I have deliberately not introduced embroidery in the preceding pages, as I considered it necessary for you to understand the basic principles of design and colour. That knowledge must now be applied to your own work, and colour plays a vital role in the field of textile art.

Texture can create differences in colour; for instance, the same hue may look dissimilar on different surfaces. Smooth, shiny fabrics will reflect the light, while the colour on matt or textured fabrics will appear dense and solid. This light and shade can be used to great effect by contrasting light and dark fabrics, laying shiny threads on matt surfaces or reversing the pile of velvets; there are many alternatives with which you can experiment.

You can see some marvellous examples of the use of colour, texture, light and shade in patchwork quilts. In the log-cabin quilt *(110)* you can see how different shades put together can change the overall effect of the final pattern when viewed from a distance. Here we have an example of a square design, but it also registers the diamond pattern. Standing close to the patchwork, you are aware of the squares and rectangles making up the design but if you move away from the quilt either the dark- or the light-coloured diamonds predominate at any one time. So an optical illusion is being created. You can also achieve this optical effect simply by placing lines of colour with irregular spacing on a background of contrasting colour, for instance red on green or black on white.

Exercise 14
To create the effect of movement using straight, vertical lines of equal length and thickness, take a piece of white fabric and either machine or hand stitch black lines, 5 cm (2 in.) in length. These lines are to run in vertical positions across the length of the fabric. Vary the width in between each line, moving gradually from wide spacing to narrow, and also let some of the lines almost touch. If you hold the fabric away from you, you will see that the straight lines appear to undulate across the surface of the material. This is an optical illusion and you can try other experiments using different contrasting colours and making other patterns, for instance spirals or circles within circles.

In my own work I prefer to start with a natural-toned silk and then apply colour as a painter applies paint to a canvas, letting the work grow. I usually have a basic colour scheme in mind, either blues or greens, for example. Then the threads are used colour by colour, tone by tone, to build up and transform the earlier background. Sometimes the colours will interreact, creating new shades which in turn will influence my next choice of colour. That original blue background may become predominantly pink or lilac or the greens turn to viridian and turquoise, but it happens spontaneously, without any preconceived idea. This is my definition of the intuitive use of colour, where the colour is allowed to grow and blend and in so doing, transform the background fabric.

112 *Movement using vertical lines.*

4 Applying colour to fabric

Having studied colour theory and considered the use of colour in landscape, it is now appropriate to look at the practical aspects of applying colour to a piece of fabric.

As a natural progression from the painting you have done on paper, you should begin with paints, dyes and paintbrushes. For all the following experiments I would recommend that you use a plain, white or natural-coloured fabric, of cotton rather than man-made fibres, as synthetic fabrics may repel the water-based dyes, leaving an effect similar to that of liquid on candlegrease. For the same reason, it is advisable to wash the fabric before use, in order to remove any dressing, as this substance, used to 'finish' the fabric, can also act as a block to the absorption of the dyes. For practising I would suggest calico, or any cheap white cotton, as suitable materials. You need fabric that is readily available and reasonably cheap, an important factor when you are experimenting. You may make mistakes and want to repeat the exercises or you may be so fired with enthusiasm that you wish to try out ideas of your own.

PAINTING ON FABRIC

Before you begin to paint, you must stretch the fabric, as you need a smooth, flat surface upon which to work. Not only will you get better results, but you will also find it easier to apply the paints and dyes. There are two ways of stretching the fabric, to prepare it for painting. One method is to stretch the material over a frame, and the other is to pin the fabric to the board. Both methods are equally valid and are used for specific techniques.

Frame method

1 You can construct your own frame by using lengths of 2.5 × 2.5 cm (1 × 1 in.) wood. This can be bought, cut to size, from your local woodyard or handicraft shop. When nailed together, the corners of the frame can be strengthened by using metal, L-shaped angle brackets. If you do not feel you can tackle this job yourself and cannot get such a frame made, the solution is to use an old wooden picture frame. This is what I use and I find it convenient to have a variety of different sizes available.

2 Take your plain piece of fabric, which has been washed and ironed, and cut it to size, remembering to cut the fabric larger than the frame. Until you are used to stretching the fabric, I would advise that you leave a 5 cm (2 in.) allowance of extra fabric around all four edges; this will enable you to grasp the fabric firmly when it is being stretched.

3 Lay the fabric onto the table and position the frame on top. Try to ensure that the grain of the fabric is running parallel to the edge of the frame, as this will help to prevent any distortion of the fibres.

4 Starting with the top edge and working from the centre outwards, staple or pin the material to the top, outside edge of the frame *(113)*. Repeat this process along the opposite bottom edge, pulling and pinning. Then, using the same process, secure the right-hand side and finally pin the fabric along the left side of the frame to ensure a smooth, flat surface.

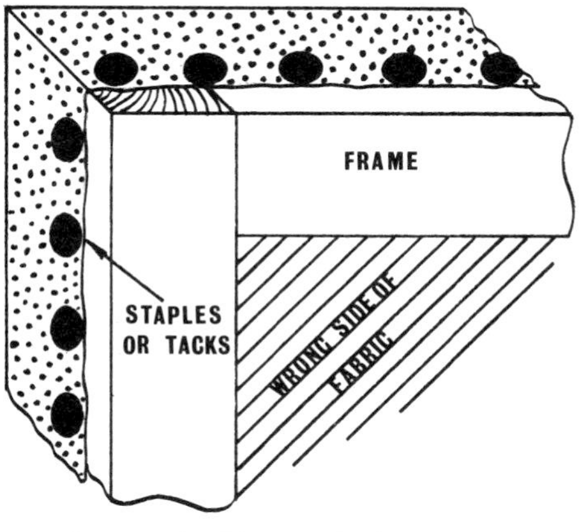

113 *Pinning the fabric to the frame.*

This method of stretching the fabric is particularly suitable for using wash techniques or for any occasion where you wish either to saturate the fabric, or to apply paint in a very liquid form. The reason for doing this is to raise the fabric away from the table area, so that you have the width of the frame between the fabric and the supporting background. This is to prevent the paint from soaking through the material and forming little pools of colour on the hard surface of the board or table, as the outlines of these pools would bleed back into the fabric and leave nasty stain marks on your work.

Board method

1 For this method of stretching fabric, you will need a drawing board, or any suitable surface capable of holding drawing pins (thumb tacks) or staples. Place a couple of sheets of newspaper over the board and then pin a sheet of clean cartridge paper on top of the newspaper, thereby securing all the papers to the board.

2 Lay the washed and ironed fabric, right side face-up, on top of the cartridge paper. Make sure that all the wrinkles are smoothed out and that the grain of the fabric is lying straight.

3 Starting from the centre of the top edge, pin the fabric down, working from the centre outwards and spacing the pins approximately 2.5 cm (1 in.) apart. Repeat along the bottom and side edges, ensuring that the material is pulled and pinned, until you have a smooth surface of stretched fabric.

This method is suitable for applying paints and dyes with the airbrush techniques. It can also be used when applying paint directly from the jar. It is a good method to use when you wish to build up small areas of colour rather than large areas of wash. I have mentioned that fabric can be stretched in this way when you wish to spray large areas of colour, but I must give one word of advice:

114 *Soft, misted effects can be achieved by painting onto slightly damp backgrounds.*

if using silk or any other fine fabric, do not stretch the material onto a board; always use the frame method. Thin fabrics, once wet, will stick to the background and staining will occur.

There are various types of paints and dyes suitable for practising with colour on fabrics, ranging from ordinary watercolour paints, gouache, acrylic paints and coloured waterproof inks, to paints specifically made for painting on fabric. When you eventually want to use colour on an important piece of work, to be framed or sold, then it is vitally important that you use colourfast, lightfast, permanent dyes, suitable for the type of fabric which you are using.

However, for your practice pieces you can enjoy yourself with colour and use any medium you wish in order to experiment with different effects.

With your fabric dry, paint in a wash well diluted with water. Apply the wash with broad, sweeping strokes and use large soft brushes, no. 15 or larger; you can even try using house painters' brushes. The aim is to achieve soft, muted effects. Try letting the colours 'bleed' into one another by painting one colour beside another; the edges will diffuse outwards and blend together. If you paint onto the fabric whilst the surface is still moist, using your paint mixed in a slightly thicker consistency, you can suggest tree trunks, distant forests on hillsides, the edges of lakes or seas blurring into mist – in fact any area where you wish only to indicate a shape *(114)*. Let the fabric dry; I use a hair-dryer in order to speed up the drying process.

When the fabric is dry, you can paint on any areas of definition. If, for example, you are trying to depict a wood in winter, wash to suggest colour tones, then add strokes of colour to suggest tree trunks or groups of pines disappearing into the forest. Let the fabric dry, then paint more defined shapes of trees and brushes; finally, you can build up the foreground with embroidery. Immediately, you have created various depths of colour and texture.

Another way of applying a wash to the background fabric is to paint onto wet fabric. To do this you need to soak your fabric in water and pin it onto the frame. Then paint on your wash, in broad sweeps of colour. This method gives a lovely soft, rain-washed look to the background, but you must work quickly before the fabric starts to dry out. You can always rewet the surface, using a fine spray of water; indoor plant sprays are good for this, but avoid overwetting or you may leave water-marks on the fabric. For this reason, do not rewet the surface using a brush. This method is particularly suitable for seascapes or large areas of sky, when you do not want too much definition.

The wash methods, either on dry or wet backgrounds, besides being particularly good for skies or sea effects, are also extremely useful when depicting backgrounds of grasslands or areas of marsh, as colour can be applied thinly, then built up stroke by stroke, and it gives a lovely foundation on which to embroider grasses, always allowing the background colour to show through. It is also useful for representing foliage background, eliminating the need for a heavy build-up of embroidery. Waterproof, coloured inks can also be used for these techniques, either in a diluted solution, or at full strength. These can give bright patches of colour over which you can embroider.

For different effects, there are other ways of applying paint. Stippling, for instance, can give unusual textural qualities. To try this you will need a selection of hard brushes, instead of the softer paintbrush. Try using oil-colour brushes,

old toothbrushes, nailbrushes, or any type of small brush which has hard, blunt-edged bristles.

The medium should be of a thicker consistency and therefore gouache or acrylic paint would be suitable; fabric dyes can be used straight from the bottle. Hold the brush at right-angles to the surface of the fabric so that the pattern derived from the flat end of the brush is printed as speckled but controlled points of colour. Stippling can also create the background effect of pebbles on a beach or massed areas of flowers. I always like to use these effects as backgrounds only, and add embroidery or detailed painting into them.

Whatever the composition of a picture, be it land or sea, the sky is an important element which can contribute its presence to a large proportion of a design. Atmosphere can be given to a composition by the treatment of the sky. It can suggest the time of day or year, show sun or snow, light or dark. The way in which the sky is coloured not only affects the mood of the embroidery, but it can also give the illusion of space or balance an area of detailed interest.

I have already explained the use of wash techniques to create gentle skies and indeed, controlled washes can also be used to depict storm clouds or heavy rain, by brushing swirling dark tones into a wet background. However, there are other effects, for instance cloud forms, where washes are not enough to suggest the softness or shape of the cumulus, which is round at the top and flat along the bottom. One method of achieving this effect is to dab the colour on with a small ball of cotton wool. This eliminates unwanted hard edges and blurs the outline of the shape. You must not, however, overdo this type of technique, or your cloud will end up looking like a snowball!

One other way of creating clouds shapes is by applying colour through cut-out stencils. To do this, take a sheet of paper and draw the required cloud form on it. Cut out the shape and place the paper over the surface of the fabric. When you paint over the cut-out, only that shape will be printed on the fabric, because the rest of the paper, from which the stencil was cut, will act as a block to the paint.

You can use many different cut-out shapes to block the surface and give

115 *The sky is an important element in design.*

simple, flat patterns, or you can lay threads down on the fabric, or stick adhesive tape to the surface to give geometric forms. Try to keep your early experiments simple and, if you are using paint, I would suggest you use acrylic, which can be thinned down with water. Do not mix too much water with the paint or it will bleed under the stencil and spoil the image of the shape. Otherwise use fabric paints which can be applied by brush, straight from the jar.

Another simple way of blocking out dye is to mix a flour and water paste. Draw around the outline of the shape with the paste and then fill in with colour. The paste acts as a resist and stops the dye from bleeding over the edge. I would only recommend this method while you are practising as I feel it is too basic for use on an actual piece of work. The same principle is used, with a greater degree of success, by outlining the shape with gutta. Gutta is a resinous liquid which forms a barrier on the surface of the fabric and is extensively used when painting on silk. The gutta, or outlining liquid, can be bought in a small plastic bottle, ready for use; the top of the bottle is then either cut to form a nozzle or, if a fine line is required, pierced with a pin. The bottle is then held upright and the gutta is drawn along the outlines of the design, and allowed to dry. The dyes can then be painted inside the outlined shapes.

Once you feel you have mastered some of the previous techniques, you may like to progress to the more advanced skills of airbrushing. This is the method I use in all my work, but it has taken many years of experimentation to reach my present standard, and still I feel that I can continue to improve and progress further. So do not feel too disheartened if at first you find the process difficult to master, or if your early results are not to your liking. Persevere with your failures and practise; you'll get there in the end.

AIRBRUSH TECHNIQUES

Precautions First stretch the fabric, as described in the painting exercises, to give a smooth, flat surface free of wrinkles or ridges. Using calico or plain cotton, pin the clean, washed fabric to the board, following the same routine as for the board method. It is much easier to spray the fabric if your board is in an upright position, instead of lying flat on a table, so it needs to be supported against a wall or some other firm upright. One word of warning: this process can be messy and you can inadvertently end up spraying not only your fabric but the area around your board. Therefore, I would suggest that you cover all your background surfaces with newspaper or buy a large piece of hardboard to put behind your stretched work. If you are not fortunate enough to have your own studio or workroom, you could try working in the garage or garden shed; or if it is a nice day, set yourself up in the garden or back yard, supporting the work against a wall.

Even if you work outside, you must still protect the wall surface, as you will not want to end the day's work with the impression of a coloured rectangle on your back wall. Not only do you need to protect the surfaces of the area where you are spraying, you also need to protect yourself. Wear an apron, overall or a man's old shirt to cover your clothes, and have beside you a plentiful supply of absorbent rags or a roll of paper kitchen towels. You also need to wear some sort of mask to cover your nose and mouth; the best types are those used in industry or agriculture for paint or crop spraying. You may be able to find them in large garden centres, but if they are unobtainable, you can use a scarf or strip or fabric. If you do use a length of cotton, put a couple of sheets of folded up kitchen towel over your mouth and nose, and then tie on the rag. The reason for doing this is to protect your throat and nose from the fumes of the paint and compressed air. Some dyes can be particularly pungent and can make you cough, or give you a sore throat, so although you may think that you look silly, it is wise to take these precautions. But do not answer the door while your mask is still in place – I have done this often and received extremely strange looks from the electricity man or coalman!

You also need good ventilation when you are using a spray gun, so always work near an open window or door, as an unventilated room can very easily be filled with fumes of which you may be unaware. The cans of compressed air are under pressure, so even when they are empty do not throw them onto a fire or bonfire, as they will explode. It is also wise to store them out of bright sunlight. It is important for your health and safety to follow these simple steps.

Equipment There are many types of airbrushes on the market, ranging from the simple to the sophisticated. The most straightforward of these is the little blow-tube, which you can buy from your local art shop. This can be used with inks or very diluted paints and dyes, and its advantages are that it is cheap and useful for simple experiments, where only small areas of colour are needed. You do, however, need a lot of puff, and can get very red in the face with all the exertion of blowing, especially if you have a large area to cover.

The airbrush I would recommend for a beginner is the basic kit brush, which is simple to use and very versatile. It also has the advantage of being able to take slightly thicker paints and dyes than some of the more advanced brushes, which have very fine nozzles and can easily become blocked. The basic kit usually contains the airbrush and hose attachment, plus some mixing jars, and you will need to buy a can of compressed air. All of this equipment can be found in the graphics departments of large art shops or model/hobbies shops.

Paints and dyes On cotton fabrics, acrylic paints can be used very satisfactorily, as they can be diluted to the right consistency for spraying. You can also use fabric paints, or, for silk, silk dyes are available. I suggest that you use acrylic paints for your practice pieces, and then progress to fabric paints or dyes when you become more proficient.

Although small, glass jars are provided with the airbrush kit, I prefer to mix my paint initially in a clean plastic margarine tub. This way of mixing allows you to see the true colour and also enables the paint to be mixed smoothly, without any lumps. Add the water carefully, a little at a time, until the paint has the consistency of single cream. It must be smooth and free-flowing, but not thin and runny or it could easily saturate the fabric. If any lumps are not removed from the paint when mixed, they can either block the nozzle or cause splattering to occur on the fabric. Once the paint has been correctly mixed, pour it into the glass jar, then screw the jar to the nozzle cap. Connect the can of compressed air, and you are ready to spray on the colour. Both the airbrush and the compressed air will come with clear instructions for their use.

116 *Removing one quarter-section of the protective paper.*

117 *Two hard-edged bands of colour.*

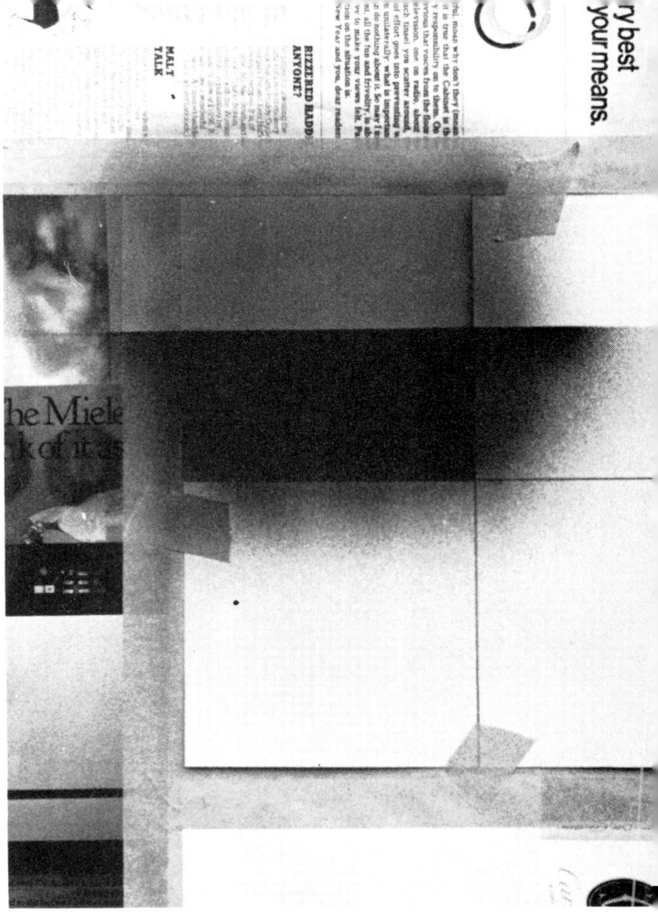

Sprayed effects You should be able to get about four samples on the stretched fabric, so take a sheet of cartridge of the same size, and cut out a quarter of the paper *(116)*. Use the remainder to protect your fabric from being marked by the dyes. Secure the paper to the board with masking tape.

Soft and hard edges

Working on the first quarter of fabric, you are going to spray two solid bands of colour. Mix up a green and a blue. Cut the discarded quarter of paper in half, and hold one half down on the fabric.

Spray blue dye across the surface from right to left until you have covered the fabric. Do not stop and start in the middle of the material or blotches will occur. Carefully remove the paper and dry the fabric using a hairdryer to speed up the process.

When dry, cover the sprayed area with paper, and hold this down while you spray the bottom half of the fabric with green dye. Remove the paper and dry. You will now have the image of two bands of solid colour, one blue, one green, with a hard edge dividing them *(117)*.

You can, by using a similar technique, blend the blue and green together, so that the two colours seem to merge together without a hard edge. To achieve this use the same process but this time instead of laying the paper flat on top of the fabric, hold it about 1 cm ($\frac{1}{2}$ in.) above the surface, thus allowing the dye to diffuse slightly into the bottom half. Repeat the process by covering the blue-sprayed area with paper, again held slightly above the surface, so that the green diffuses slightly under the edge and merges with the blue. Remove the paper and dry. The result shows two colours blending together in the central section. The joining of the colours give a soft rather than a hard edge *(118)*.

118 *Blending two colours together to give a soft, diffused edge.*

119 *Sprayed diagonal lines.*

Diagonal lines

I have already mentioned that diagonal lines give an illusion of vitality to a piece of work and apart from stitching, you can also spray diagonal, vertical and horizontal lines. On your practice sample, turn the protective paper round, clockwise, until you have covered the previous experiments. Hold a piece of cartridge paper or thin card diagonally across the fabric. Starting from the top left-hand corner, aim the spray along the edge of the paper, from top to bottom. Move the card along and spray the next diagonal *(119)*. Try to keep the distance between lines as equal as possible.

Once you have completed this sample, you can try varying the widths of the lines. Reverse the diagonals to make lattice-type patterns *(121)*. You can spray horizontal or vertical lines; the variations are endless.

If you want to use more than one colour, then you will need to mask out the previous one before respraying. If you do not mask out, then the overspray will ruin the first colour. This can be overcome by cutting out a slot from a piece of thin card, making it a fraction longer than your diagonal line. Then line up the angle and position it over the unsprayed area, thereby protecting the other colour. Use this method for horizontal or vertical lines.

Cloud and sky effects

To give the effect of rays of the sun breaking from a bank of clouds, use the straight edge of a sheet of thin card. Make sure that the card covers the entire length of the sky or you will have strange vertical angles appearing amongst the clouds. Direct the spray along the edge of the card, as this gives a softer image than spraying directly onto the fabric. The card can be held to give the effect of horizontal bands of clouds, layered one upon another, or a piece of card with a torn edge can be placed at a slight angle to create the illusion of windswept clouds.

120 *Sprayed diagonal lines emphasized by embroidery.*

121 *Sprayed lattice shapes.*

122 *Selective spraying.*

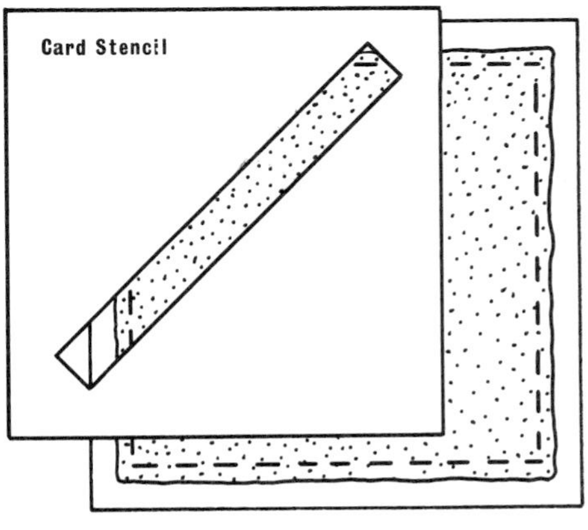

122

121

123

124

When spraying clouds I would suggest using a very pale colour instead of white, as white can have the effect of being too hard or harsh. The only time white can be used is if you have other bright colours in the design. For instance, a hot sunny day with brilliant blue sky can balance the whiteness of clouds. You can cut out cloud shapes from a larger piece of paper and, holding the paper above the surface of the fabric, spray through the negative or cut-out shape *(122)*. This will give the impression of a cloud, without it having a hard edge. You can then move the card around and build up an area of cloud using a subtle range of colour.

You may want to give the effect of a gradual colour change, moving from dark to light. To do this, hold a strip of thin card about 1 cm ($\frac{1}{2}$ in.) above the surface and lightly spray the fabric, moving smoothly from left to right, then from right to left. Do not oversaturate the fabric by trying to achieve a darker tone in one stage. It is much better to spray and dry, and then if the colour needs to be more intense you can overspray again. Gradually move the card down the sky, spraying gently until you have covered the area required. You can introduce other tones using this method, and as long as the card is held above the surface of the fabric, you should not get any hard-edged lines. It is always advisable to let the colour fade out as it reaches the land or sea, for this gives depth and solidity to the horizon line.

These instances are related specifically to the more representational interpretation of landscape, but all these techniques can be used to create abstract designs and once you are familiar with them you will be able to develop them to suit your own particular style.

Stencils The stencil is a development of the early cloud shapes mentioned

125 *A gradual colour change from dark to light.*

123 *Sprayed cloud effect.*

124 *The four completed exercises.*

above; it is a method of painting through the spaces of cut-out shapes. You can use it for clouds, trees, fields and rivers, and a whole multitude of shapes. You use it not only for spraying on colour, but also for blocking out colour. The points to remember are:

1 Do not make your shapes too complicated, or you will have difficulty in cutting them out.

2 Always leave enough spare paper around the shape so that it acts as a buffer between the design and spray and in doing so, protects your fabric from picking up unwanted dye.

3 If the stencil or paper is laid flat on the fabric you will print a hard-edged image.

4 If the stencil is held slightly above the paper, the sprayed shape will have a softer edge.

If you are spraying up a landscape, you may not want to have a large number of small stencils, as these can be easily mislaid. A method I use is to leave one edge of the stencil attached to the surrounding outside paper. If, for instance, I wanted to spray the design in *fig. 127* I would cut the horizontal lines but leave

them attached to the outside edges, rather like a series of flaps; they can then be lifted, or laid flat, as required *(128)*. Where you have three sides meeting an outside edge, such as in the sky or foreground field area, you would cut two sides, leaving the other attached to the paper border. The following section explains the procedure for making up a landscape stencil.

Landscape stencil
Take an accurate tracing from your design drawing; mark in all the important main lines, and also put in the outside perimeter of the design. Place the tracing on a flat sheet of cartridge paper and trace through, until you have an exact copy of your tracing, on the drawing paper. Also pencil in a 1 cm ($\frac{1}{2}$ in.) border all around the outside of the design. This border gives an added allowance to the sprayed design, as often additional machine embroidery can distort and pull in the sides of the fabric. It also allows for any dribbles or sudden spurts of dye when you first depress the spray, as dye can come out with a sudden rush. The border allowance is only to be used if you are covering the outside edge with either a card or fabric mount. If, however, you wish to extend your design, or have the plain fabric showing around the sprayed inner landscape, then you must cut the stencil to the exact measurements of the initial tracing and not cut out the border.

Cut along the hill lines, leaving the outside edge attached to the paper surround. When all the lines have been cut, fold back the shapes to ensure that each section is attached to an outside edge, and stick a small piece of double-

126 *Letting the colour fade out towards the horizon line of the sea.*

127 *A paper stencil.*

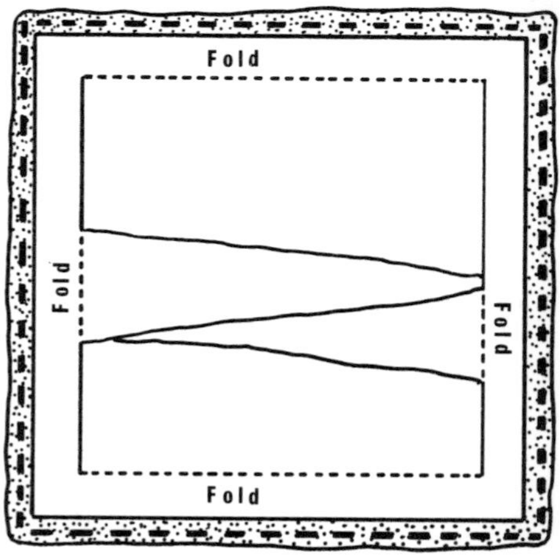

128 *Lifting the stencil flaps.*

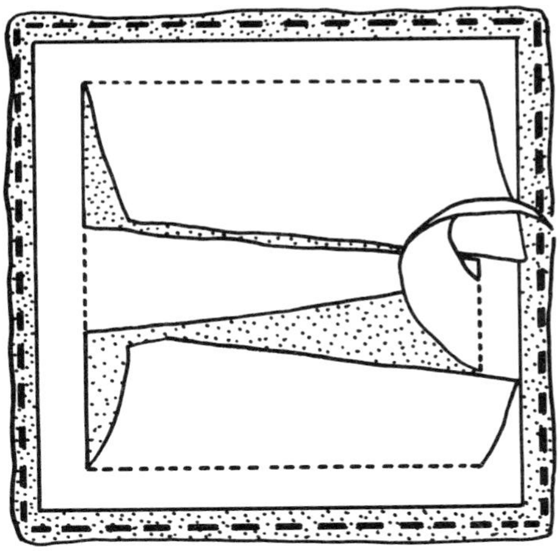

sided adhesive tape to the back of the shape. The tape lightly holds the stencils in place while spraying. Once a section has been sprayed, always remove the double-sided tape before replacing over the newly sprayed area. If you do not remove the tape, it can pick up dye, leaving an imprint on the fabric's surface. This, of course, completely spoils the sprayed surface.

Using this method, you can lift the stencil and spray a specific colour onto a specific area; once sprayed, you can fold back the paper to cover the shape, then lift another flap, and so on.

When spraying up a landscape background it is relevant also to consider aerial perspective, and the lighting within the landscape.

Aerial perspective This is a means of indicating relative distance:

1 Far-distance objects and land masses are palest and contain the least amount of detail.

2 Middle-distance tones are slightly darker, although still subdued in colour, while objects such as trees are less detailed.

3 Near objects and foreground areas are darker and more detailed.

Therefore, if you wish to create an illusion of depth in a representational picture or even if you want only to suggest simple landscape planes, you can, by the use of this formula, give a background of colour tones which can be applied at the spraying stage. The perspective can be further emphasized by the application of embroidered detail.

129 *Aerial perspective.*

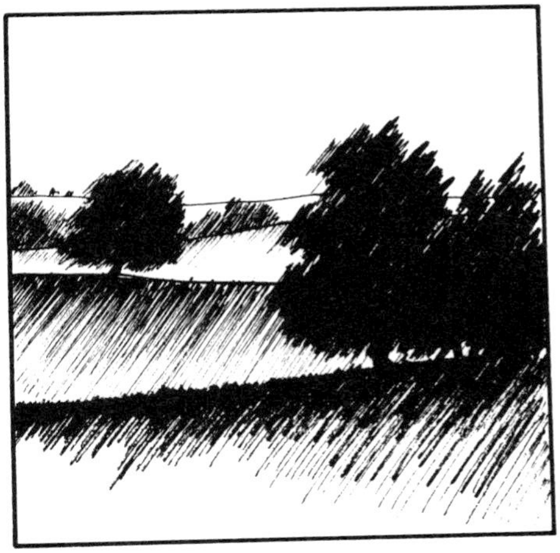

130 *Planes of aerial perspective.*

Lighting within a landscape When spraying up a background, you should think not only of the seasonal colour tones, but also of the changes of light within a landscape, caused by the direction of the light source and the time of day or night. The sun, for instance, may be shining from the left side of the scene and casting shadows to the right side of objects. If it is midday and the sun is directly overhead, the tops of objects would be in bright sunlight, while the sides would be in shadow *(131)*. At midday when the sun is high, the landscape is bright and sunny, but at sunset, the lighting in the same landscape changes. The sky is highlighted and the landscape, especially along the horizon, is shadowed.

If you consider the same view in winter, the light is frontal: it is coming from the front of the scene, as if from over your shoulder as you stand facing the landscape. The foreground snow would therefore be lighter and brighter, whilst the sky would appear darker *(132)*.

These small considerations will help to give depth and atmosphere to your work and if planned at this stage, the landscape colour can be sprayed in to create this illusion. So, by planning your areas of light and shade you are not only spraying in colour, but giving yourself an interesting background upon which you can add embroidery. The embroidery gives texture and detail to the work, but the sprayed colour gives added interest and depth.

131

132

131, 132 *Lighting within a landscape.*

5 Machine embroidery techniques

Machine embroidery can be used to create texture, line and colour. The needle can be used as a pencil is used for drawing, so there is a freedom and spontaneity not found in hand embroidery. Although it has all these attributes, the great disadvantage of this embroidery process lies not in the technique, but in the application of machine embroidery and its apparent difficulties, which lead to many people abandoning the process in the introductory stages.

I hope that this chapter will help those who have tried, and in desperation turned away from, machine embroidery, for it is an exciting and versatile medium. It does need practice to learn to control the machine, in order to make the marks you want to make. *You* must learn to control the machine, not let the machine control you. Once you have learnt to overcome your fear of this inanimate object, you will find a new freedom in your work.

EQUIPMENT

Before embarking on a course of machine embroidery you will need the following equipment:

A sewing machine, preferably with a swing needle
A circular hoop or frame
Small, sharp, pointed scissors
Machine embroidery threads, no. 30

Sewing machines Although an ordinary, straight-stitch machine can give a basic machine line, the swing-needle machine, in which the needle swings from side to side, has many more uses, from the simple securing of a piece of applied fabric to a background, to the freer technique of using the zigzag to cover large areas of texture. The fully automatic machine is the most expensive, and this not only does straight stitch and zigzag but also a variety of different embroidery patterns, particularly suitable for dress embroidery.

Whatever your choice, you must ensure that the machine is suitable for *free*-machine embroidery. The feed or teeth must be capable of being either dropped or covered. The dropping of the teeth is usually done by pushing a lever, which lowers the metal teeth below the surface of the plate. Instructions for this will normally be in the instruction manual. Some of the older machines may not have the means of lowering the feed, and if this is the case a cover-plate will be needed to cover the teeth. Some of the new computer-controlled machines may also not be suitable for machine embroidery as the constant changing of tensions may damage the delicate mechanisms. If you are definitely interested in machine embroidery it would be better to use a machine specifically for that purpose, rather than damage your normal dressmaking one. Second-hand, reconditioned machines can be bought, and a simple swing-needle, flat-bed machine, would be most suitable. A flat-bed machine is a machine which is set into the base to give it a flat working surface. My own machine is an industrial flat-bed and it is set into a work bench, so I have a solid, flat, working surface which supports my embroidery hoops and frames. If you are not able to set your machine into a bench or table and you only have a free-arm machine, then you will need a clip-on frame, to fit round the arm and give a flat working surface. The two problems with the clip-on frame are firstly that it can be difficult freely to move the

133 *Basic equipment for machine embroidery.*

134 *A design can be worked sideways to fit under the arm of the machine.*

embroidery hoop around, and secondly that it is often awkward to get at the spool.

Embroidery hoops For free embroidery, it is important that the fabric is tightly stretched, so you will need a hoop or frame. Metal embroidery hoops are the best as they hold the fabric taut in the frame, but if you are unable to buy a metal one, a wooden hoop can be used. If using a wooden hoop, it is advisable to bind the inner frame with thin strips of clean fabric. This not only helps to hold the fabric in place but also prevents the hoop from marking the material. (This is especially important in dress embroidery, where the continual moving of the hoop could cause ring marks.) However, in my own work I find the best way of stretching the fabric is to staple it over a small wooden frame, either one which has been made specifically for a project, or else an old, flat, picture frame. The advantage of this method is that it enables the fabric to be stretched drum-tight; in fact, it should ping like a drum. If you do decide to use this frame method, do ensure that:

1 The frame is flat enough to go under the machine needle.
2 You are able to get into the centre of your embroidery from at least one direction, even if it means you have to work sideways or upside-down. It is very easy to work away on some area of texture, only to find that a gap of plain fabric refuses to be filled in the centre. This can be avoided by always checking that the size of the frame, from its centre to the outside edge, is not larger than the distance from the needle to the machine neck. You should also make sure that your areas of embroidery are in reachable sections. For example, in *fig. 134*, although the frame is too long to allow the needle to reach the centre point, in this design it is not too important, as all the textured detail is in the foreground and therefore the design can be worked sideways. This is slightly difficult, but it is a problem which can be overcome.

Pointed scissors Small, sharp, pointed scissors are essential, as you will need to cut off threads close to the surface of the fabric, and it is extremely annoying to find that your scissors are either not pointed enough to get into the textured surface or not sharp enough to give a clean cut.

Embroidery threads Machine embroidery cotton can be bought in two thicknesses, no. 30 and no. 50. No. 30 is most commonly used and is better for beginners, as it has less tendency to break, and also gives a richer, thicker stitch. No. 50 is more suitable for fine fabrics such as thin silk or organdies, but I would

not advise beginners to use this, as the thread has an annoying habit of breaking frequently, and this can be very frustrating to someone trying to cope with the technicalities of machine embroidery.

SETTING UP THE MACHINE FOR FREE BASIC RUNNING STITCH

The feed must be lowered or covered and the presser foot removed. The machine is threaded on the top and in the spool with machine embroidery cotton. It is a good idea whilst you are practising to use different colours on the top and in the spool, as this will help you to check the tension.

Check that the spool is running in the right direction as some run clockwise, others anti-clockwise. The machine instruction book will give you the necessary information.

The fabric to be embroidered must be larger than the hoop or frame as this makes it easier to pull the material tight. The right side of the fabric is uppermost in the frame, so that as you are working at the machine, the right side is facing upwards. (The exception to this rule is when you wish to use thick threads, such as perlé or metallic threads, in the spool; in this case the wrong side of the fabric must be uppermost.)

Pulling the material tightly as you work around the hoop, screw up the frame, or stretch and staple onto the wooden picture frame. It cannot be emphasized too much that the material in the hoop or frame must be as *tight* as possible. If the surface is not as taut as a drum, then the machine will not stitch once the presser bar has been removed, as the fabric will be pulled up with the needle; remember to check the fabric's tautness at regular intervals, since it may loosen as you are working on it.

The sewing machine needle must be fine and sharp and you must be prepared to change it frequently. You can test the needle for bluntness by gently rubbing your finger under the needle's point (make sure the machine is switched off when you do this); you will be able to feel if the point is sharp or worn down. The needles you use should be a no. 11 English size (70 or 80 continental). I find that no. 80s are most suitable for machine embroidery as 70s tend to break more easily when working at speed. If you find that the needles for your machine are sized differently then try to obtain the size corresponding to a continental 80. Check that you have inserted the needle in the correct way.

Place the hoop or frame under the needle and lower the presser bar. This is extremely important, and a procedure often forgotten by beginners and experts alike. If the presser bar is not lowered, you will have no top tension and this will cause the machine to jam below. If this happens you will have a tangled mess of threads underneath your embroidery, or the threads may even jam around the spool case and will have to be cut away. You could even tear the fabric – so please remember to lower the presser bar.

Once the bar has been lowered, the cotton from the spool is brought to the top of the work by holding the top cotton and making one stitch, turning the wheel of the machine by hand *(135)*. Before you start to embroider, hold down the two ends of the cotton for the first few stitches; these can then be cut off. It is not necessary to darn in the ends of threads in this type of free embroidery, as they do not unravel.

135 *Cottons in position on the top surface of the fabric.*

The frame can now be pushed in any direction under the needle; even small circular lines can be stitched, which cannot be done when a normal presser foot is in place. The length of the stitch is determined by how fast the hoop is pushed in relation to the speed of the machine. The length of stitch lever, which is normally used with the presser foot, now no longer controls the stitch length as the feed has been lowered and the foot removed.

Both cotton tensions must be checked. For a basic, surface running stitch the cottons need to be of equal tension on both sides of the work, and they need to be slightly looser than average. On some machines the spool tension is loosened by adjusting the tension screw. It is important not to turn the screw too far or it may drop out, and you will end up scrabbling around on the floor looking for this minute object. If the tensions are too tight, a pulled stitching line will result which will pucker the fabric.

To remove the frame from under the needle, set the needle at its highest point, lift up the presser bar and by slowly turning the wheel, gently pull the top cotton through the take-up lever, and slide the frame away from the machine. Never pull the frame away sharply, as this will result in the needle breaking or bending.

Now that you know how to set up the machine for a simple running stitch, it is possible to advance to more interesting stitches, by altering tensions or width of stitch or by using thicker or metallic threads.

OTHER STITCHES

Whip stitch Machine embroidery cotton is used on the top and in the spool. The top tension is now made slightly tighter than usual, while the bottom spool tension is made looser. Move the frame around slowly as this allows the bottom thread to whip itself up around the top thread, giving a neat, corded stitch.

Exaggerated whip stitch Again, use machine embroidery cotton no. 30 on the top and bottom; this time, however, the top tension is very tight and the spool tension very loose. If you move the hoop slowly, the thread pulls up into a high corded stitch, but if the hoop is moved quickly, especially in circular movements, then a decorative button hole type of stitch is attained, which is useful for creating large areas of texture.

Whip stitch and exaggerated whip stitch are the stitches I most frequently use, as with them I can create both the linear and the textural qualities I require in

36 *Whip stitch.*

137 *Decorative use of satin stitch, showing the technique of appliqué. By Angela Dickinson.*

embroidery. Although these techniques may appear simple, absolute control of the machine is needed to achieve maximum usage of the stitch. These stitches are discussed in detail in the section on the application of machine embroidery to landscape (page 104).

Satin stitch Your machine needs to be set to zigzag stitch. Satin stitch can be used in the same way as the basic running stitch, but it gives a wider line. When used with metallic thread, as described below, it gives a rich and decorative effect. If used with normal machine embroidery cotton, both on the top and in the spool, it gives thick lines; used freely it can give interesting textural effects. Used on open-weave materials such as scrim, it can give the same quality as pulled fabric, especially when the top and spool tensions are tighter than normal.

USING UNUSUAL THREADS

Perlé Machine embroidery cotton no. 30 is used on the top, but perlé thread, either the thicker no. 5 or the finer no. 8, is wound by hand onto the spool. The top tension is very tight and the bottom tension is extremely loose. In some instances, when a very textured surface is required, the screw and tension band on the spool case can be partially or completely removed, so that the thread can flow loosely. If you like the effect of perlé, then it is advisable to buy an extra spool case which can be used solely for perlé or other thicker threads, so that you do not risk damaging the tension spring on the spool case required for normal use.

As the thick thread will not now be pulled up through the fabric, you will need to work with the *wrong* side of the fabric uppermost in the frame *(138)*. In other words, you are working upside down, so that the bobbly stitch will build up on the *right* side of the fabric *(139)*. If the hoop is moved slowly, then the stitch becomes more textural; if the top tension is tightened, then the effect is also more exaggerated. You can use metallic threads or stranded silks in the same way as perlé.

138 *Working on the wrong side of a perlé sample.*

139 *The finished right side of the perlé sample.*

If you eventually decide to use a combination of work with perlé thread and other types of machine embroidery, I would recommend that the perlé embroidery is done first; once this has been completed, the hoop is removed, then placed on again, this time with the right side of the fabric uppermost; you can then proceed with the free-machine embroidery.

Metallic threads These threads should be worked in the spool, and they can be wound directly from the reel to the spool. Care should be taken whilst winding flat-sided Lurex, to ensure that it is wound flat and not twisted. The machine embroidery cotton on the top of the machine should be as near as possible in colour to the Lurex in the spool. Again, the right side of the work should be face downwards, with the top tension tight and the spool tension loose. It may even be necessary to remove the tension screw. As you work on the *wrong* side, you can check that the top tension is tight enough – you should be able to see a similar effect to that of a metallic whip stitch. In other words, you should be able to see particles of metallic thread on the back of the work. This ensures that only the metallic thread is showing on the right side.

LACE WORK

Use a closely woven fabric which will not easily fray, as shapes will need to be cut into the material. The free-embroidery method is used, with machine embroidery cotton on the top and in the spool. The tensions are normal to slightly tight.

Three rows of running stitch or a free zigzag stitch are worked around a simple shape. The shape is then cut out with sharp, pointed scissors and lines of running stitch are worked across the open space, so making fragile chains which can then be embroidered into with more lines *(140)*. The edges of the cut fabric can be neatened up with a zigzag stitch. This is basically the same principle as darning, but you can achieve some very interesting and decorative patterns, especially if large areas are treated in this way until you have a lacy effect.

This technique could successfully be applied to areas where you require open, frothy effects such as foam and snowflakes. You will, of course, need to adapt the scale of the embroidery to suit the scale of the work, but this type of technique can be very effective, especially in more abstract pieces.

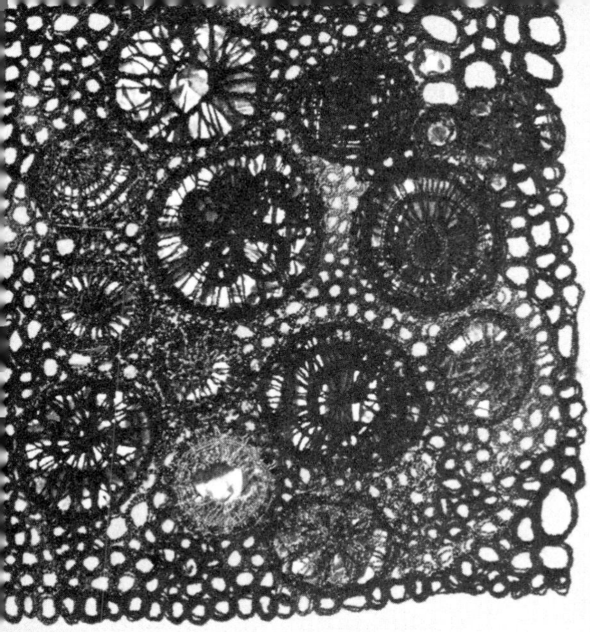

140 *Lace work.*

141 *Trees worked in drawn threadwork.*

DRAWN THREADWORK

Open-weave materials such as hessian, linen or scrim are needed for this work; some of the weft or warp threads are then completely removed. Use the free-embroidery method with machine embroidery cotton no. 30 on the top and in the spool, with the tensions normal to tight; set the machine for zigzag stitch. The thicker threads in the fabric are caught together, giving thicker lines and therefore a stronger effect than in lace work *(141)*.

DRAWN FABRIC WORK

The machine is set up in exactly the same way as for drawn threadwork, and the same type of open-weave fabrics such as scrim are used; however, this time, no threads are removed but the zigzag stitch catches and pulls together the warp and weft threads.

Both drawn threadwork and drawn fabric work can be applied to landscape, and can be used to suggest tree trunks, fences and hedges; if used in conjunction with whip, perlé or appliqué, the effect can be strong and vigorous.

APPLIQUÉ

For this technique you will need to work with the foot on the machine and set up for zigzag stitch. Tensions will be normal, as for ordinary dressmaking. The fabric shape is cut out and tacked to the background. The zigzag is then worked all around the shape to secure it to the base fabric. Interfacing can be ironed on the back of the material before the shape is applied. This not only strengthens the fabric but helps to prevent undue fraying of the edges. This is the simplest method and the one generally used for panels. The zigzag can either be left as a slightly open stitch, or can be worked over with a wider, closer stitch, to give more of the effect of satin stitch. The finished result very much depends on whether or not you wish to emphasize the edge of the shape. For example, a slightly more open zigzag will blend in with the surrounding tones and textures, whereas a close satin stitch will catch the light and even appear heavy and solid. Even if the thread colour is matched to the fabric, it will be more noticeable, therefore the type of zigzag used will very much depend on the required result.

CUT-THROUGH WORK

Two or three layers of fabric are placed on top of each other like a sandwich, the principle being that successive layers are cut away to show the underneath colours. If the shapes to be cut are small or complex, then the free-embroidery method can be used; otherwise, on large and simple shapes, it is easier to work with the presser foot on the machine.

The stitch can either be running or zigzag, but the length of stitch needs to be short. A short length of stitch makes it easier to manoeuvre the presser foot around the curves than a long length of stitch would.

Mark the design on the back of the fabric, making sure that the grains of all the fabric used are running in the same direction, as this will prevent any puckering. Securely tack or pin the layers of fabric together to prevent underneath fabrics from slipping and distorting.

Work on the back of the material, stitching around the drawn lines of the shapes to be cut away. When the various layers have been stitched together, very carefully and working from the front, with small sharp scissors, cut away the unwanted fabrics between the stitching lines, to expose the different colours underneath the surface layers. Once all the cutwork is completed, then the edges can be neatened by a wider zigzag if required.

42 *'Façades' by Angela Dickinson, showing* *ppliqué techniques.*

This particular technique, using successive layers of fabrics in different tones, would be very suitable for depicting stone walls or pebbled beaches; in fact, it would work well for any area where numerous small shapes of different colours are needed to create the illusion of a coloured, multi-faceted surface.

QUILTING

English quilting You will need three layers of fabric: the top fabric upon which the design will be seen, a wadding material and a light cotton backing. The wadding is placed between the two layers of fabric and all three are pinned together. You may find it easier to draw the design onto the cotton backing and work from the wrong side. However, whether you work from the back or front, the design should be one that can be worked with a presser foot on a machine using a running stitch. It is easier if you work with continuous lines, as this saves the constant sewing-in of ends of cotton – these all need to be darned in at the back of the work.

Italian quilting For this you need two layers of fabric – a top material and a light cotton backing – and also quilting wool. Use a running stitch, with the presser foot on the machine. It is necessary to form a channel through which the wool will be threaded. To do this, use either a twin needle, or, if this is not available, stitch two parallel lines, approximately 3 mm ($\frac{1}{8}$ in.) apart, until all your design has been machined with small channels.

Working from the back and using a blunt-ended quilting needle or a tapestry needle, thread the wool through the channel. Where you have a curve, the quilting wool must be taken to the outside of the work, so make a small snip in the backing and gently ease through the wool. This stops any 'pulling' around the curves.

Trapunto quilting This type of quilting gives padding in selected areas only. The top fabric should be pliable, such as fine wool or viyella, while the backing layer should be firm and resistant to stretching, such as a stiff, mercerized cotton poplin. If the layers of fabric are reversed, then the padding will be more apparent on the back of the work.

If the shapes are small, then the free-embroidery method can be used; otherwise the presser foot must be employed. The shapes must be enclosed and a running stitch machined around them. The cotton backing is then slit and the stuffing is pushed into the shapes. If the shapes are small, they can be stuffed with animal wool, or if large, with kapok. When all the shapes have been padded, sew up the slits.

These three quilting techniques are, I think, particularly suitable for large, bold statements and lend themselves to hangings and bed quilts. The quilted shapes can obviously suggest the contours of the land and a combination of the three techniques could be used. For example, English quilting could represent hills and fields as broad shapes of colour, while the Italian quilting could give the detail of a ploughed field or hedgerows. Once the technique is acquired, it is up to the individual to interpret, according to the dictates of design and style.

6 From embroidery into landscape

Machine embroidery is a fast and effective way of creating colour and texture. Its adaptability makes it suitable for translating even the most complex of designs from paper to fabric. Before you can develop your own style, you must learn to control the machine. This can often take time and patience, but I assure you that the results are worth the effort.

If you are a beginner, concentrate on the basic, surface running stitch until you have overcome any fear of the machine, which can initially seem too fast and uncontrollable. You need to get the 'feel' of the machine and must learn to co-ordinate the movements of pushing the hoop with the right amount of foot pressure controlling the speed. It is rather like driving a car – the experience seems daunting at first but then becomes enjoyable.

Once you feel you have mastered the machine, then test your control by setting it up for whip stitch. Before starting, check that your fabric is still taut in the hoop; if not, retighten. When the fabric is under the needle, make sure that the presser foot is down. Support the hoop with both hands and if possible, rest your elbows on the table as this relaxes the wrists, and makes for easier movement of the hoop.

Keeping the lines fluid and free, try to build up an even, corded stitch, then push the hoop a little faster, so that the stitch becomes more open and the thread lying along the surface of the fabric is noticeable. When you feel you have mastered this technique, try to build up small areas of linear texture, about 5 cm (2 in.) square.

Exercise 1

1 Embroider one area with tight and close stitches so that you have an attractive, dense texture.

2 Make another area in open and loose stitches, by moving your frame backwards and forwards at a slightly faster speed. Use two different-coloured threads, one on the top and another in the spool, for an open, bobbled texture.

3 Using an exaggerated whip stitch, made by tightening the top and loosening the bottom tensions, build up another texture using small circular movements. If worked with variegated cotton, this gives a lovely foliage texture.

4 Repeat these last three techniques, but this time use a zigzag stitch combined with the whip stitch.

You should now have six examples of different types of texture *(143, 144)*, and can experiment further by mixing these together, using one colour at first and then introducing other colours. The textures can lie side by side, or overlap or intermingle. See how many different effects and textures you can obtain.

When you have satisfied yourself that all the textural possibilities have been explored, move on to the controlled drawing in line of a simple object.

Exercise 2 – control

1 Try to draw with the needle a simple, six-petalled flower. Work from the centre outwards until all the petals have been formed. Machine in the stem and leaves and finally work the centre of the flower. Working this last ensures that any untidy ends or lines are covered, and neatens the finished result.

143 *Three samples of whip stitch.*

144 *Samples of whip stitch worked on the zigzag setting.*

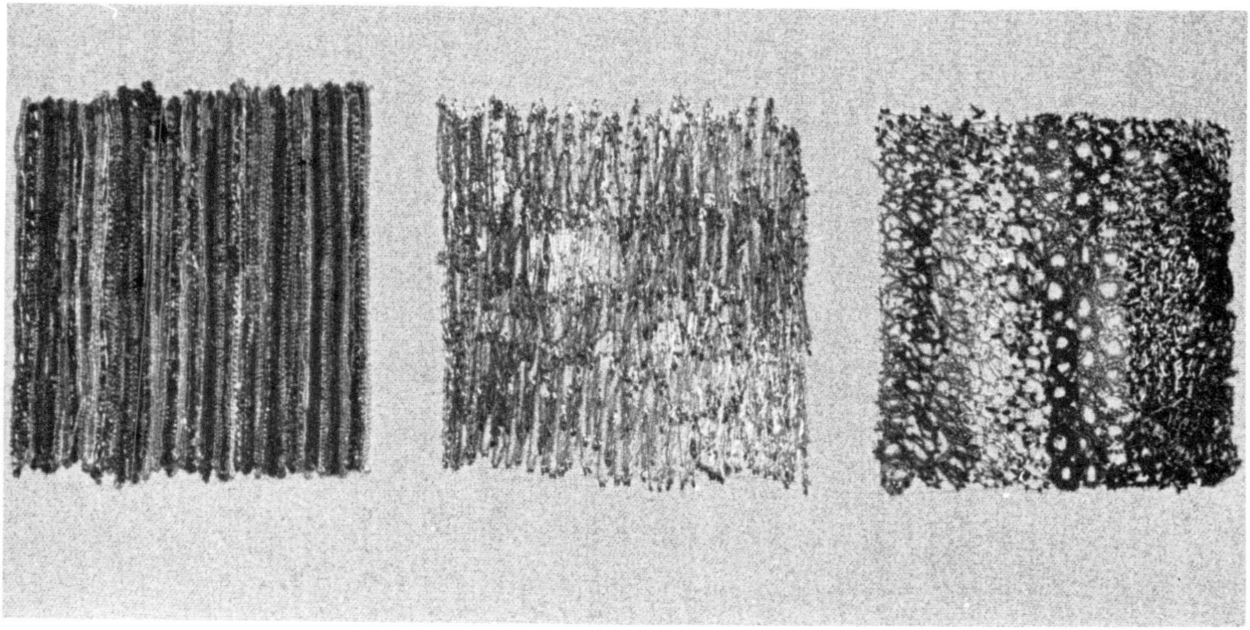

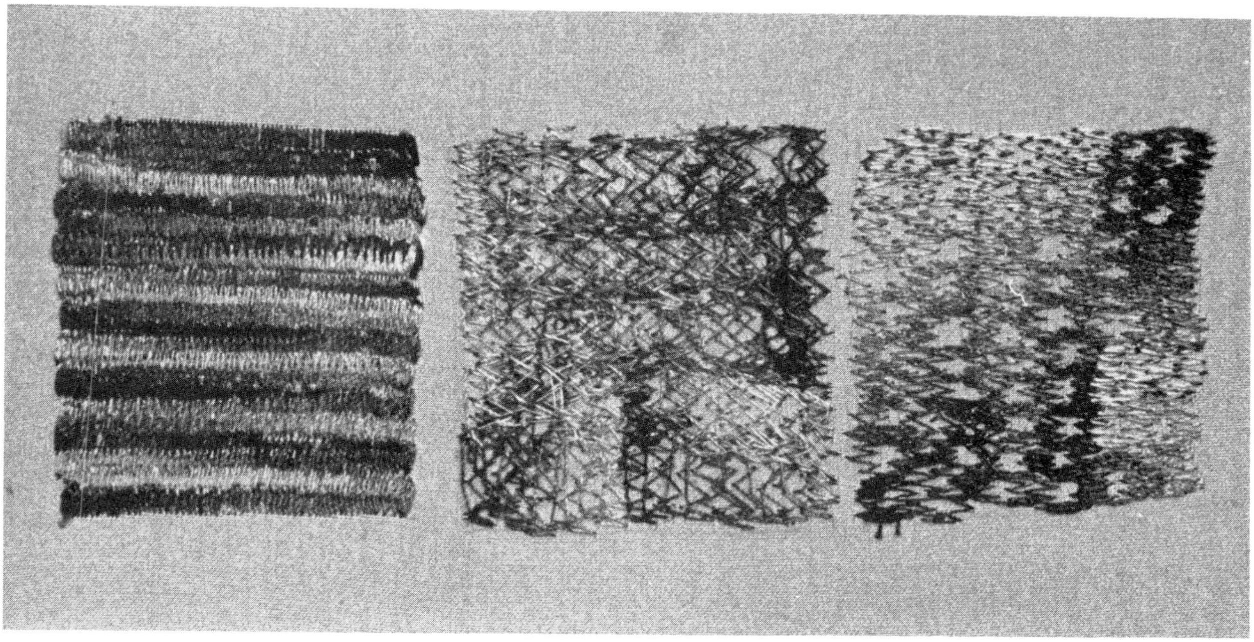

2 Draw a tree in summer. The outline shape can be very simple, but the illusion of summer is created by the colour and texture used. You could experiment by trying different approaches to the tree. One could be a simple outline shape, filled in with solid whip stitch *(145)*; or you could use exaggerated whip stitch with two different shades of green, one on the top and one in the spool, to give a more textured effect.

Try embroidering leaf-shape clusters using variegated machine thread to give light and dark shades to the foliage; or embroider in dark areas of colour, to represent shadow, then work over the top of these in other shades of green to soften the hard edges of the dark colours and to give the impression of shadows glimpsed through heavy foliage.

145 *A tree worked in solid whip stitch.*

146 *A sample showing how separate trees can be differentiated whilst using continuous texture.*

147 *Tree trunks seen on flat ground.*

3 Using the same tree techniques, try to create a tree in winter. Obviously the colour used will be different: first embroider a simple outline tree shape, filled in with blue, instead of green, so that the colour, not the foliage, suggests the season. Try to draw a bare tree, keeping the lines simple and stark, or one with a minimum amount of foliage. Remember that you are suggesting a tree in winter, which is to be interpreted by the use of line, texture and colour.

4 Embroider a clump of trees and try out different ways of grouping them together. They might stand in line on the horizon, so that the trunks will be obvious but the colours of the foliage will blend together. If the trees are along the edge of the meadow in the mid-distance, the colour changes from one tree to another will be more noticeable and you will have to recognize that change within the embroidery. This can be indicated by a drawn outline, or a distinct change of colour from one tree to the next, even though the texture and embroidery is continuous. Again, the texture of one tree may be different from that of its neighbour, and you can show that difference by changing the type of stitch you make, by tightening or loosening the tensions *(146)*.

In a cluster of trees, some may stand behind others and you need to be able to suggest whether they are on flat ground or on a hill. If they are on flat ground, you will be aware of the colour and texture of the foreground trees and may see more trunks than trees *(147)*. If the trees are standing on a hill and the viewer is looking upwards, then the mass of foliage covering the hillside, perhaps broken by a few visible trunks, will be more noticeable, so you will need to use a variety of shades of machine cotton to suggest this large area of coloured texture.

Be prepared, when covering large areas of interest, to keep changing the colour of the threads; I like to thread up possible colours onto my spools before I start, so that I only need to change the colours of the reels, without having constantly to rewind the spool.

You are now able to expand your vocabulary of machine techniques and can interpret the uses of texture to suit your own style. The next stage is to create larger areas, such as fields, using only machine embroidery.

148 *An embroidered field showing foreground detail and texture.*

Exercise 3

First of all, try embroidering a series of hill lines from the horizon, through the middle distance to the foreground. These lines must suggest the linear structure of the landscape and must, by the use of colour and thickness of line, convey the illusion of nearness and distance. You must only use line and not introduce solid shapes. Do not forget that the further away an object is, then the lighter and finer the line must be; in the foreground, the lines will be thicker and darker.

The previous exercise showed how distance can be achieved by the use of colour and diminishing texture. This same principle can be applied to the following exercise, which uses four squares with sides of approximately 10 cm (4 in.).

Exercise 4

1 Try to capture the quality of a field seen in the distance. Remember that the colours will be pale, texture will be minimal and the illusion can be further emphasized by keeping the embroidery lines horizontal, as this flattens and diminishes the surface.

2 The second 10 cm (4 in.) square should create the impression of a field in the mid-distance. In this section a little more texture will be introduced, the colours will be slightly stronger and some small areas of detail may be observed. You can achieve this by breaking the horizontal lines with some small verticals and adding touches of colour to represent flowers.

3 The foreground or close-up section will contain most colour and texture and forms or structures of grasses and flowers will be recognizable. You will find it easier to embroider if you start at the top and work down, embroidering the background grasses before you add the detail of flowers. Look at these squares and notice the differences in tone, texture and scale.

4 In the final square, use all three techniques to illustrate a field, giving the illusion of recession, diminishing the scale, texture and colour. Obviously your treatment of this square needs to be handled carefully, for although it is the same size as the others, you will need to put more thought into the proportion and breakdown of areas. You also need to think about how to blend the three sections together to give a smooth joining of the diminishing tone and texture. If you were unhappy about the success of the previous three squares, you can correct the balance in the final one.

This exercise has shown how atmosphere and depth can be created with machine embroidery by relating the application of texture to the specific use of colour and form. Machine embroidery has many possibilities, but it must be seen as an integral part of a work and not just as another surface technique.

COMBINING HAND AND MACHINE EMBROIDERY

Although my own interest lies in machine embroidery, I often use some hand techniques to enrich the textural areas, or to give extra light and shade. This

149 *An embroidered field showing recession.*

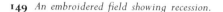

151

lightening of a work's surface is achieved if silk threads are intermingled with cotton; if the silk threads are stitched by hand, then the difference in texture gives added interest.

If the work is to be embroidered mainly by machine, then areas of hand embroidery need to be selected carefully, as the addition of too much hand embroidery can make the work appear heavy.

Linear stitches such as couching, stem stitch, long and short stitch or the running stitches – for example plain, back stitch, brick or double – all blend in well with machine embroidery. You may have favourite stitches with which you would like to experiment; but whatever the stitch, it must be in scale with the rest of the embroidery. Seeding, for instance, is delicate enough to be integrated into the design, and blended with open machine embroidery, it can be used to depict tufts of grass receding across a field. It is also a useful stitch for fading out or softening a hard edge, where a diffused line is preferred.

If you are interested in an abstract interpretation of landscape, then texture can be an important element in the composition. A bolder use of the machine stitch, incorporating drawn thread or drawn fabric work or with heavy areas of texture, can combine well with textured hand stitches such as bullion or french knots, wheatear, vandyke or herringbone stitches.

Whatever your style of preference in design, if you wish to use a combination of hand and machine embroidery, the techniques must be complementary to achieve the overall result. You are aiming for a *total* effect, in which all the techniques used work together to form a whole.

150 *Hand embroidery techniques have been used to enrich the textural areas and give extra light and shade. Silk threads are intermingled with cotton, using a free interpretation of straight stitch and long and short stitch.*

151 *'Foxtail Lilies', by Milly Stevens, showing an abstract interpretation of landscape.*

152 *Two details from a series of panels commissioned by the National Farmers' Union, Stratford upon Avon, and worked by Eleri Mills. The panels are in appliqué and hand stitching on a background of brushed and sprayed acrylic paint.*

USING MACHINE EMBROIDERY WITH PAINTS AND DYES

Exercise 5

Before you embark on your own work and choice of subject matter, try to interpret in your own way, using fabrics, dyes, paints and threads:

A storm
A sunset
After the rain
A hot, sunny day

A storm Think about the essence of the storm – the dark tones of the sky and landscape, lit, perhaps, by flashes of lightning. Is the storm at its height, or is it about to erupt? These thoughts will help you to decide on colour schemes and background tones to be sprayed onto the fabric. The application of embroidery needs to emphasize further the feeling of tension or depict the illusion of the storm's violence. Trees and grasses are blown around and nothing is static; the appearance can be one of movement. Machine embroidery is particularly useful for this, as diagonal lines can swiftly be built up to give moving areas of texture.

A sunset In this example, colour is of the prime importance and the sky can dominate the land. Think of sunsets over the sea, reflected in the oceans, or flat expanses of meadows bathed in golden light. Imagine the sun setting behind a group of trees, lighting the horizon but silhouetting the trees against the skyline. These trees would be dark and if machine-embroidered, the texture of the foliage could be open enough to allow the colour of the sky to show through. Dark foreground detail against the coloured background could look very dramatic.

153 *Interpretation of an approaching storm, showing strong contrasting areas of light and dark.*

After the rain In this example, colour yet again sets the mood, from the soft, cool tones of a land in the early spring, to the bright clarity of colours after a summer shower. The skies can change from pearly grey to pale turquoise or vivid blue, depending on the time of day or season. The embroidery needs to emphasize the rain-washed tones and capture the light of wet leaves and grasses; this can be achieved not only by the colour of the thread used, but by its substance: silk in particular, both as a background fabric and in threads, helps to enhance subtle changes of light.

A hot sunny day Colour and texture create this illusion. Warm colours with an abundance of yellows, oranges and some red, portrayed against a brilliant blue sky, immediately react on the senses to give an impression of heat. The landscape would be full of foliage and flowers, so plenty of texture would add interest to, and balance, the colour. Foreground detail could show an abundance of flowers and grasses, such as poppies, daisies or cornflowers. Choose flowers that either suggest summer or enhance one of the brighter tones of the sprayed background; for example, cornflowers reflect the blue of the sky and introduce that tone into the greener landscape.

154 *Interpretation of a sweeping, rain-washed sky and landscape.*

155 *Creating the illusion of a hot, sunny day, with a golden corn field, poppies and cornflowers and strong shadows under the trees.*

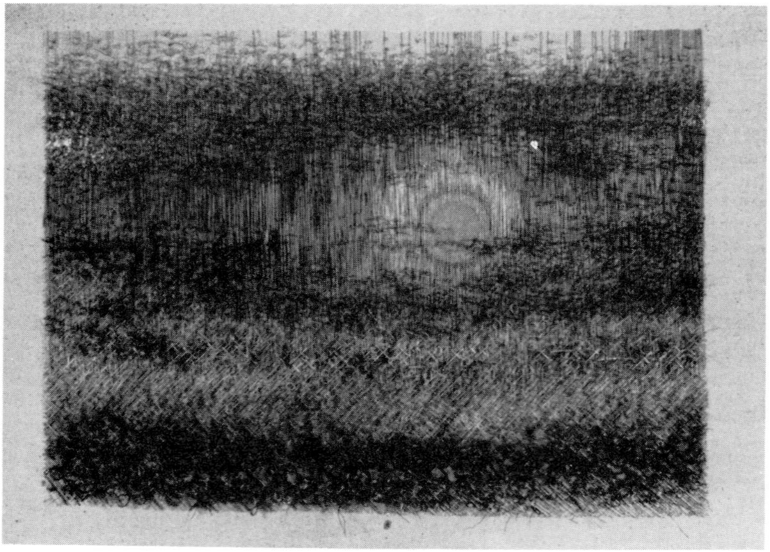

156 *'Indian Summer', hand embroidery by Jean Draper. Transparent fabrics are used as a background to many layers of cross-hatched straight stitches in very fine threads. The colours used are blues, greys and golds. Small loops all over the piece give a hazy effect to the colour. The base of the picture has torn scraps of fabric, knots and loops of cotton and fine metallic threads.*

157 *'Coastal Textures', hand embroidery by Jean Draper. Transparent fabrics are used as a background to the many layers of cross-hatched straight stitches, loops and knots in a variety of fine threads, perlé cottons and fine metallic threads. Scraps of iridescent fabric are suspended above the thick texture. The colours used are greys, greens, beiges, creams and white.*

All of these examples are only suggestions, to help you to bring observations from landscape into your work to create a mood or illusion. You can experiment with some of the stitches mentioned in this chapter and combine them with hand-worked textures, but remember that the stitchery used is only as important as the design, construction and colour of the total piece of work. You should not let the stitchery overwhelm the design, but allow it to work with the background. Your embroidery was conceived as a whole, therefore the finished piece should read as a totally integrated work – your personal statement of a landscape-inspired concept.

7 Mounting and presentation

A good piece of work can be ruined by bad mounting and presentation. It cannot be emphasized enough that the way in which you present your work reflects upon the finished result. It can end up looking tatty and untidy, or professional. The presentation need only be very simple, but if it is done well, that simplicity succeeds in enhancing the finished work.

STRETCHING WORK

Before the work can be framed, it must be stretched to ensure that the surface is absolutely taut and free of wrinkles and creases.

If your work has been stapled over a wooden frame, the fabric should already be under tension, but as machine embroidery can sometimes pull shapes out of true, check that all straight lines are still straight and re-adjust as necessary. Remove the pins or staples from the area where slackness occurs and retighten, making sure that you do not in the process distort other shapes or lines.

If, however, you have been using a hoop which has been applied and removed many times, then the fabric will need to be stretched by a different method. Ironing is not recommended once the embroidery has been completed, as it will flatten the surface texture.

For this method of stretching you will need a drawing board or wooden surface into which you can stick drawing pins (thumb tacks) or staples, and several sheets of blotting paper. Note that the drawing board or other surface should be larger than the fabric to be stretched *(158)*.

1 Lay the sheets of blotting paper onto the board and thoroughly wet them with clean water.

2 Place the embroidery on top of the blotting paper with the right side of the work facing upwards.

3 Working from the centre outwards, gently smooth out the work to eliminate the larger bumps.

4 Begin at the centre top and pin or staple the fabric along the top edge, ensuring that the grain of the fabric is straight and the design is not being distorted.

5 Pull the bottom edge in the same way and secure so that the fabric is now taut.

6 Repeat this process along the other two edges until all the fabric is fastened to the board. It should now be as flat and tight as a drum skin, without any wrinkles or creases showing.

7 Allow it to dry naturally, preferably left in a warm place overnight. Do not remove any pins or staples until the surface of the material feels completely dry.

Once the work has been stretched it must be secured to a base, either by lacing over a piece of plywood or by stapling to a wooden frame.

Wooden-frame method This method is suitable if the work is large and card mounts are not required.

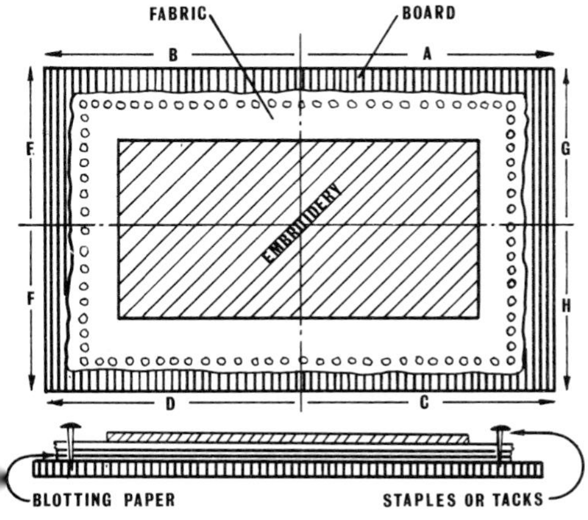

158 *Stretching fabric.*

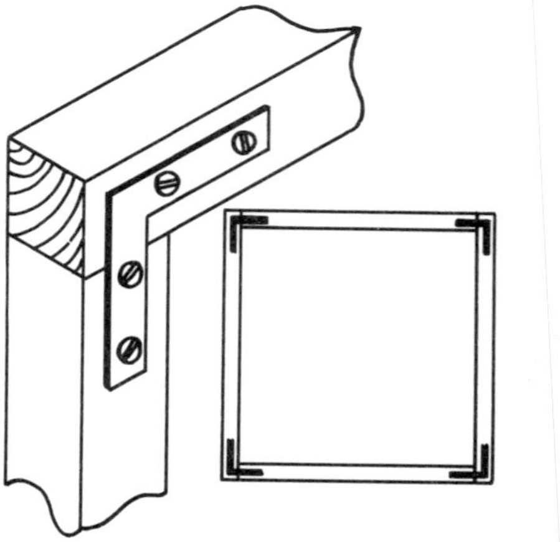

159 *Making a wooden frame with angle brackets at the corners.*

1 You will need a firm wooden frame made by joining four pieces of wood, measured to size, with screw-on angle brackets to give additional strength to the corner sections *(159)*.

2 Place the fabric with the right side face down onto a table or other flat, clean surface. Lay the frame on top of this and position, until the straight edges of the frame are parallel to the straight edges of the embroidery.

3 Working from the centre of the top edge, carefully secure the fabric to the back of the frame with a few drawing pins (thumb tacks). Repeat on the opposite edge and then on the two sides.

4 Check at this stage that the embroidery is still straight and has not been pulled out of shape. Once the design is in its correct position then you can staple the fabric onto the frame, removing the pins as you staple each side.

5 You will be aware of the excess bulk around the corner sections but it is advisable neatly to fold in the extra fabric, rather than cutting it away, and staple down *(160)*. Cutting can often result in frayed edges which become visible once the corner sections are pulled under tension. A lining fabric can be hand-stitched to the back of the work to neaten and finish its appearance.

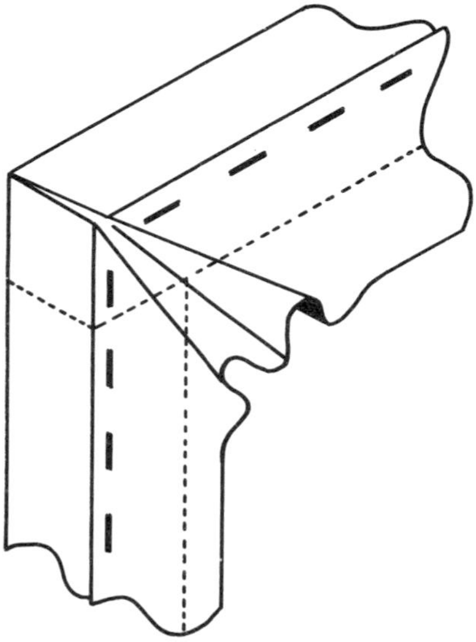

160 *Folding corner sections.*

Stretching over a board This method is particularly suitable if the finished embroidery is to have a card mount, which will cover the staple holes made in the excess fabric.

1 You will need a piece of plywood about $\frac{1}{2}$ cm ($\frac{1}{4}$ in.) thick. The size of the outer edge of the wood needs to be a little larger than the actual embroidery size, but smaller than the size of the outside of the card mount *(161)*.

2 Place the plywood on top of two books which raise the height of the work above the surface of the table. With the extra height from the books, the frame can be pushed downwards towards the table, putting extra tension on the fabric and so tightening the surface.

3 Shoot in a few staples along each side to hold down the work and stop it from slipping; then staple down each side.

4 When the work is firmly secured, remove the wooden frame.

5 Lay a clean sheet of paper on a flat surface and onto this place the work face downwards. Trim away the surplus fabric to within 4 cm ($1\frac{1}{2}$ in.) of the plywood.

6 Fold in the side flaps over the plywood and, working from the centre outwards, lace up the sides, using a darning needle threaded up with strong linen twine or fine string *(162)*. Make a loop to begin the lacing, rather than a knot, as under the pulled tension a knot may tear through the fabric. Another point to remember when lacing is that when you have brought the needle through the material, you should take it back under the thread. This provides a slight point of friction which makes it easier to tighten the lacing.

7 When the side pieces have been laced, fold over the top and bottom flaps and repeat the lacing in the same way, turning in the corners as neatly as possible.

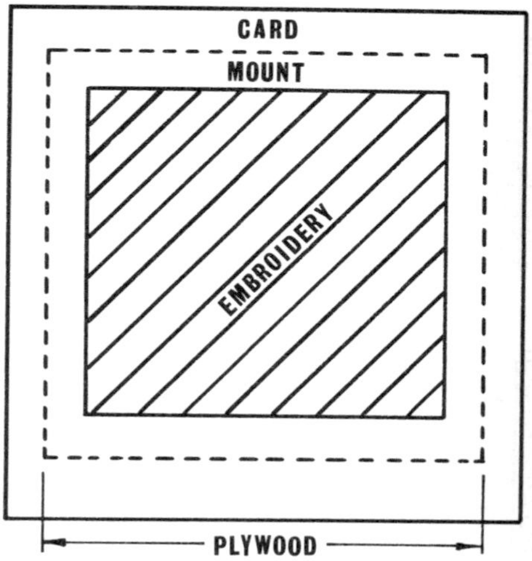

161 *The proportion of plywood to card mount.*

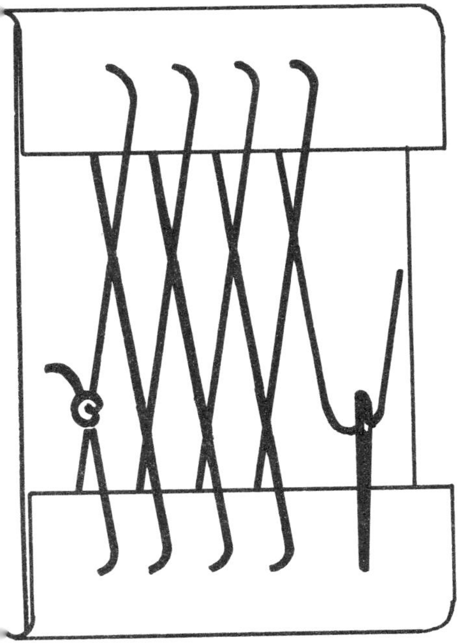

162 *Lacing.*

Once your embroidery is laced, it is advisable to remove the staples from the front side of the work. If you leave the staples in the fabric, they may rust and cause future damage to the embroidery or its card mount.

If you want to stretch a number of small experiments or samples, then, as well as the lacing technique, work can also be stuck down to the back of the board. If the work to be mounted is small, then hardboard or thick card can be used.

1 Position the hardboard onto the back of the stretched work, and starting from the shortest side, carefully stick down one edge using a rubber-based adhesive. Pull the opposite side taut and stick down.

2 If you have any excess fabric at the corners, cut away a small rectangular shape to reduce the bulk.

3 Stick down the other sides, pulling gently as you do so, to remove creases and tighten the surface of the work.

4 Finish off by either slip stitching or gluing a lining to the back, or presenting the work in a card mount.

MOUNTING

Mounting and framing not only finishes the work but neatens up edges and gives a sharpness and clarity to the perimeter of the design. You can take your work to a framer and have it professionally framed and I would recommend this for large pieces which have been stretched using the wooden-frame method described earlier.

If your embroidery is small or has been laced over a board or strong card, then you can attempt to mount your own work. You will need some equipment for this and also a clear, flat area upon which to lay your cutting board.

Card Mounting board or matt can be purchased from good art shops or graphic suppliers; try to get 'six-sheet' card – this denotes the thickness of the card. Anything thinner will be too floppy and thicker card will be difficult to cut. Before you buy the card, check its surface by angling it against the light source. You will be able to see if the surface of the card is marked or flawed. Thumbprint marks can often be seen in the corners if the card has been frequently handled, so do check that your piece is pristine.

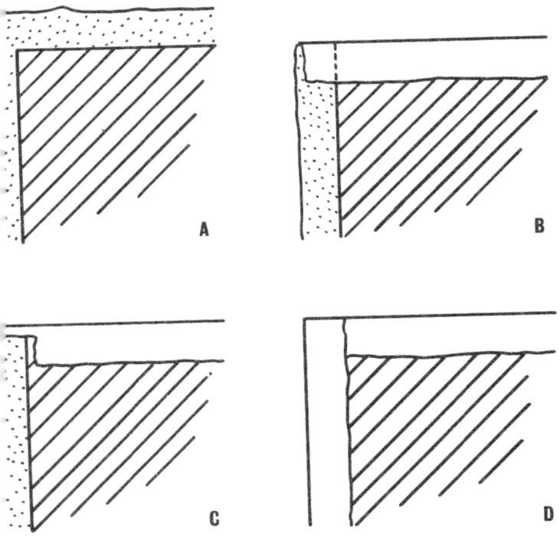

163 *Gluing and cutting corner sections.*

When choosing a sheet of card, it is advisable to take with you either the piece of work or some samples of the fabric and threads used; this will help you to match up the colours. Do not estimate, as you may buy the wrong colour. Something that looks right in the shop under artificial light may seem a different colour when placed beside the work in your own environment. You might, for instance, want to match up an embroidery which is predominantly blue; after purchasing a sheet of blue card, which you *think* might be the right colour, you could return home and place it beside the finished work only to find that against the strong colours of the embroidery, the card now looks grey or brownish.

I keep a stock of card in shades of different colours but my initial choice from this selection often has to be reviewed because of these subtle colour changes.

When you have made your final selection, handle the card carefully – try to

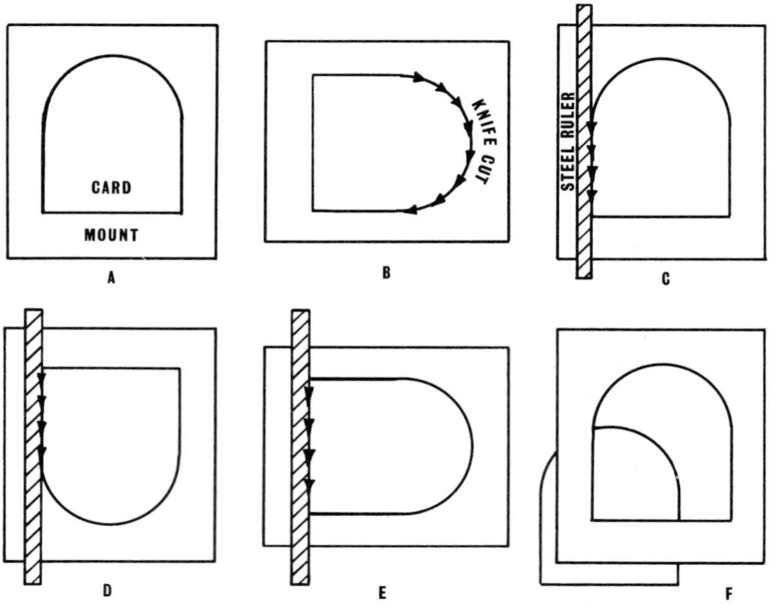

164 *The cutting sequence.*

remember how easily it marks. I have found that the least possible damage is caused by holding the sides of the card against the flat of the palm.

Sometimes you may come across an assistant who will not wrap up a single sheet of card, thereby exposing the corners to damage. If this happens it is worth buying two sheets and turning them coloured side face inward, as this protects the vulnerable surface and they only need to be lightly taped together.

Knives and rulers It is essential that a sharp blade is used for cutting *at all times*. There is a variety of cutting knives on the market which can be bought with replacement blades. The type most suitable is the craft knife with a continuous disposable blade. This has been developed in the last few years and makes it economical to keep a sharp blade at all times. Such knives can be purchased from good art suppliers or craft and hobbies shops.

Plastic or wooden rulers can be used for marking out the lines to be cut, but do not use them as edges for cutting, as sharp blades can easily slice into the wooden or plastic edge, and so ruin not only your ruler but your straight line. You could also very easily cut your hand if the blade bounces over the ruler. Use either a steel ruler or a ruler with a metal straight edge, to give a firm support when cutting.

Marking out The width of the card used as a mount should be in inverse proportion to the size of your work. For example, the larger the piece of work, the narrower the mount, whereas smaller pieces of work can often benefit from wider mounts.

Draw out the shape to be cut on the reverse side, so that any mistakes can easily be erased without spoiling your card. You must remember that you are working with a mirror image. Always allow plenty of extra card and be prepared to trim down to the correct size afterwards, as you can often get thumbprints on the edge of the card.

Mark out the design on the reverse side of the card. The proportions of the mount should be considered. A useful rule for a rectangular mount is to make the top and two sides the same width, while the bottom is generally 2 cm ($\frac{3}{4}$ in.) wider. For example, if the widths of the top and two sides are each 7 cm ($2\frac{3}{4}$ in.), then the bottom would be 9 cm ($3\frac{1}{2}$ in.).

Cutting You need a cutting board or surface upon which to cut. On no account cut out on a table, as it will be ruined by deep scratch marks. You should use the board on the back of a large block of cartridge paper, a sheet of hardboard, or an old drawing board. Alternatively, you could buy a self-healing cutting mat, upon which you can make up to 20,000 cuts while it still retains its smooth surface. These are excellent but expensive and can be obtained from graphic suppliers.

When placing the ruler, always lay it to the side of the drawn line where it protects your mount. If the knife slips, it will cut only the piece of card you wish to reject, not your mount *(164)*. Cutting the straight lines is reasonably straightforward. The problem is how to avoid shooting past the corner, so begin by placing the knife at the bottom corner and make a small indentation with its point. Move up to the top of the line, checking that the ruler is still lying straight and correctly aligned. Insert the knife and make one continuous, flowing cut, from top to bottom. As you hit the bottom corner, you will hear and feel the knife register against that initial indentation and will know not to continue the cut any further.

Turn the card in a clockwise direction and line up the straight edge to repeat the cutting process along all four sides. If this is done correctly, the central section should drop out easily; if not, do not on any account try to push the card through, as this only tears the edges. Normally, it is the corners that are holding it in place, so make some secondary cuts in each corner using the point of the knife. This should be sufficient to free the middle section.

Many pieces of work benefit from a double mount. For this you would need to repeat the procedure by cutting out another rectangular shape approximately 1 cm ($\frac{1}{4}$ in.) larger. These two shapes are laid one on top of the other, with the larger internal rectangle placed on top of the smaller, to give a stepped effect. You can use card of the same colour, two different colours or two tones of one colour. Fix the two together with an appropriate glue and allow to dry out thoroughly.

Cutting curves

On the reverse side of the card, mark out the shapes with a compass. If possible, you should endeavour to cut the curve in one movement, although this cannot be done with a complete circle. Every time you stop and start you interrupt the flow of the cut, so as you reposition yourself to continue cutting, remember to leave the knife in the curve rather than removing it each time. This ensures a smooth, continuous curve or circle.

If you want to cut a shallow curve or arch shape, be like a golfer practising his swing without hitting the ball, and practise the movement of cutting the curve without making contact between the knife and card. Proceed when you feel you can make the cut from one end of the curve to the other in a continuous sweep.

One point to remember is that it is easier to match up straight lines to curved cuts, rather than curved cuts to straight lines. So, if you are cutting a mount that contains curves and straight lines, such as an arch, always cut the curves first.

Bevelled edges

There are various cutting tools available for the cutting of bevelled mounts.

165 *Curved mounts.*

166 *Wrapped bands.*

However, speaking from experience, this is quite a difficult task and is perhaps best left to a professional framer. One thing you must not do is to try to cut a bevelled edge with your ordinary cutting knife and steel rule, as you will only succeed in cutting your fingers.

Bound frames and borders In my own work I have developed a technique of using silk-bound bands and borders, which provide a link between the areas of fabric and card. These bands are cut from the same card mounting board and can be of whatever width you require.

I use thin strips of card about 3 mm ($\frac{1}{8}$ in.) wide and cover them with silk threads. You could, however, apply this technique to thicker bands covered in wools or heavy cotton threads; use the material to suit the style of work.

I use thin bands of card which are cut to precision with a craft knife and steel rule, as described above. Strips of double-sided adhesive tape are applied to the reverse side of the card. The protective covering of the tape is removed section by section as the wrapping proceeds. Do not peel off all the covering before you begin the binding, or fluff and dust will adhere to the sticky surface of the tape. This may cause the wrapped threads to slip as they are no longer held securely by the adhesive tape.

Silk or cotton threads are then wrapped by hand over the card bands, the sticky tape ensuring that a constant tension is maintained *(166)*. The wrapping must be done carefully and methodically, so that the threads do not become twisted. The colour of the thread can be changed by using a small piece of double-sided tape to fasten off and restart each colour.

Corner pieces can either be left unbound and painted to match the colours of the threads, or separate strips of card can be cut and butted up against each other to form an angle. If you decide to use separate bands, then it is advisable to put a small piece of double-sided adhesive tape at the end, on the right side of the card, as well as the normal strip on the back. This helps to hold the threads when starting or finishing a band.

The extra width which is added to every band by the addition of the thread, although small, will need to be allowed for in the card mount. Therefore a very fine sliver of card should be cut from the inside of the mount. As it is extremely thin, it need only be taken from one side and the top, not from all four sides, as this would make too loose a fit. If you are assembling a mount containing an arch, do not try to cut a sliver of card from the curve as it is virtually impossible to do so evenly. Instead, remove the excess from one straight side and the bottom horizontal.

The completed band can then be attached by registering its position on the card mount; working on the reverse side, stick small pieces of brown gummed paper over the card and binding *(168)*.

Another type of fabric frame is made by covering wide bands of card with fabric. Cut out the card band to its correct size and width, using a steel rule and cutting knife. Make a template of the card shape and pin it onto your fabric, making sure that the grain of the material is lying parallel to the length of the card. Cut out the fabric, leaving a border all around as in *fig. 169*. Turn in the side flaps and lace together, then repeat along the length, until the card is covered with a smooth wrinkle-free surface of fabric.

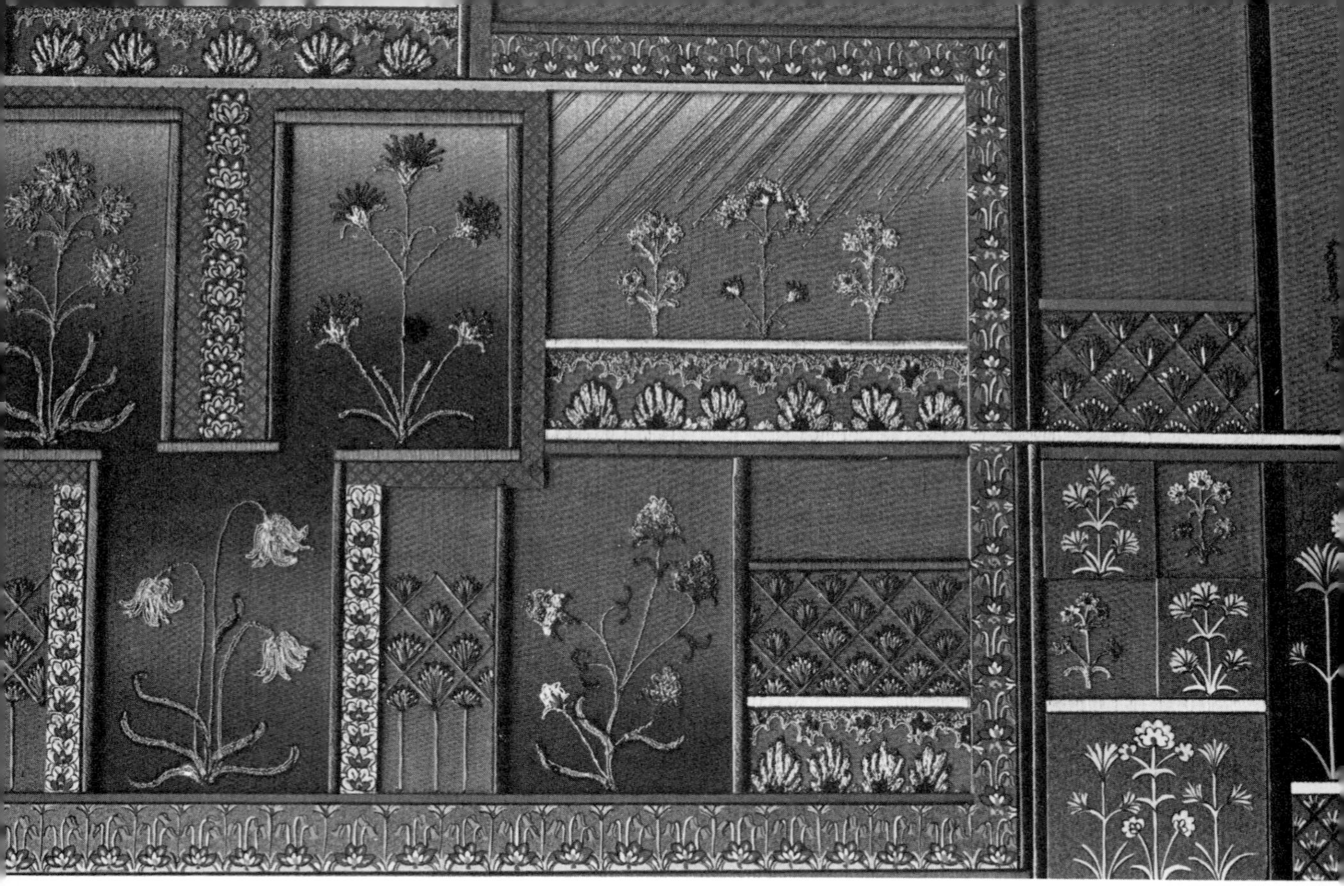

Any fabric can be used, but my own preference is for silk, as it not only looks good but also reflects the light and gives interest to the border. These covered bands can be arranged to give simple borders or you can make them more intricate, using double or triple bands *(170)*. They can be sewn together along the edges as for English patchwork, or can be stuck onto the area of excess fabric surrounding the stretched embroidery. The bands serve the same purpose as the card by covering and neatening untidy edges; they can be left as they are to form the frame, or you could cut a card mount as previously described, then inset the completed work in a simple frame.

167 *Detail of an embroidery showing silk-wrapped borders.*

Finishing off the back You should now have in front of you your piece of embroidery, laced and stretched, and your cut card mount. The assembly stage is next and as this is fairly complicated, I have given step-by-step instructions.

1 Register the mount on the work so that it fits correctly.

2 Take the discarded piece of card you have cut out from the central section of the mount, and replace this so that it exactly fits the shape. When you are sure it is in place, carefully remove the outer card mount, leaving only the central section covering the embroidery.

3 Apply four small areas of contact glue to all four outside edges of the work *(172)*.

4 Apply glue, matched to the same positions on the reverse side of the card mount. Allow to dry.

5 Assemble by gently placing the mount in its correct position over the embroidery. When you are sure that they are correctly aligned, press down

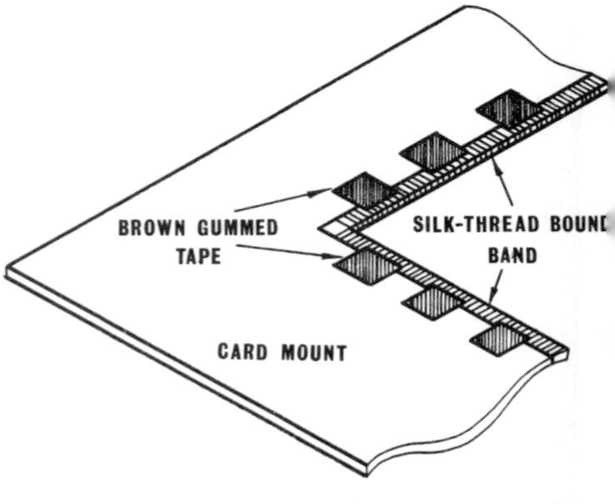

168 *Registration of bound bands (reverse side).*

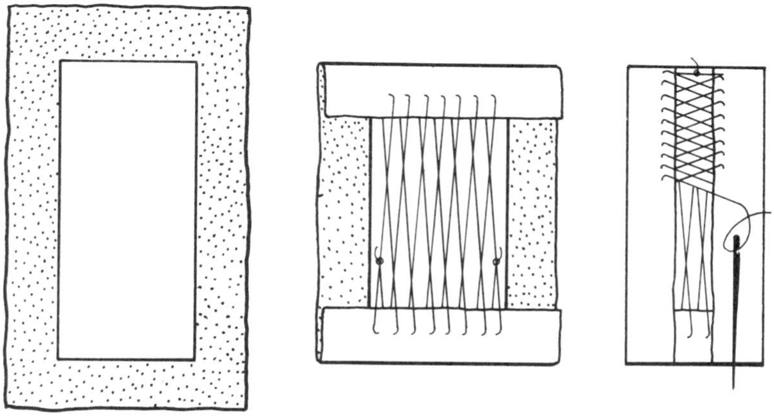

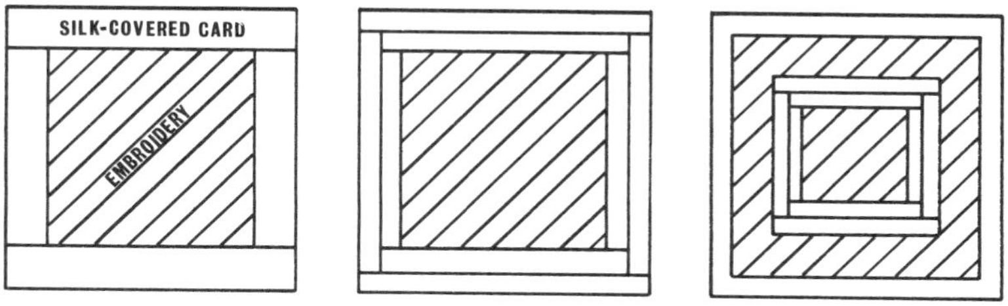

169 *Covering card for a fabric frame.*

170 *Border variations using fabric bands.*

171 *'Aureola', a design showing curved corners cut to fit couched borders. Inlaid frame by Stewart Warren.*

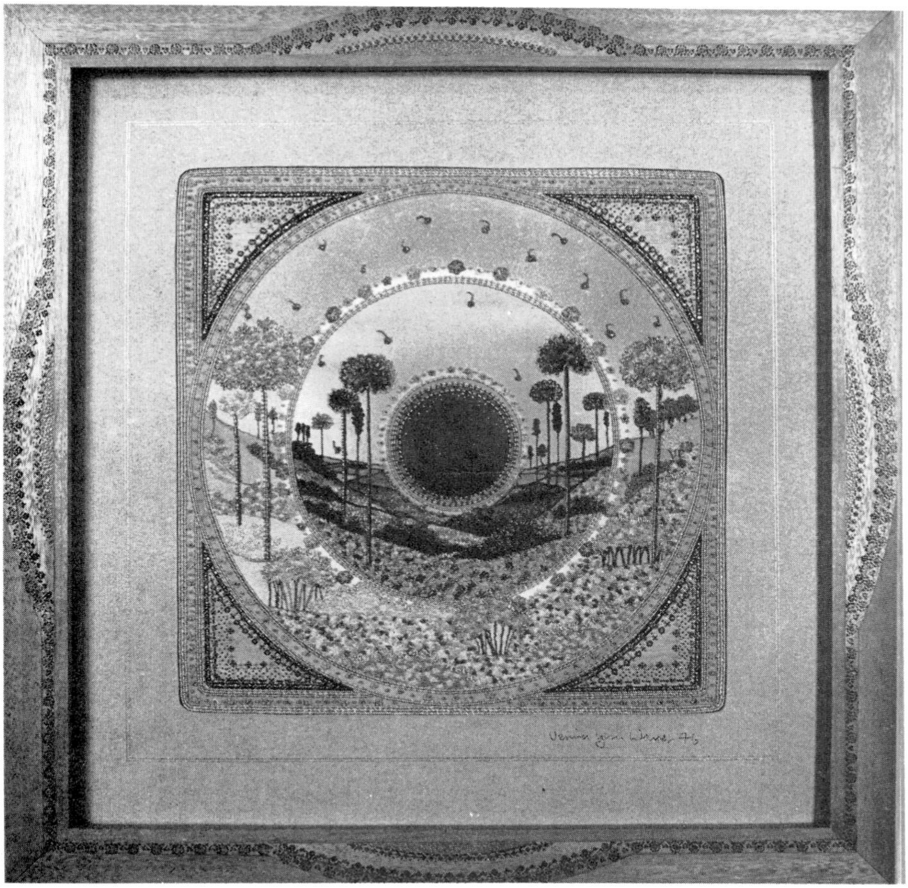

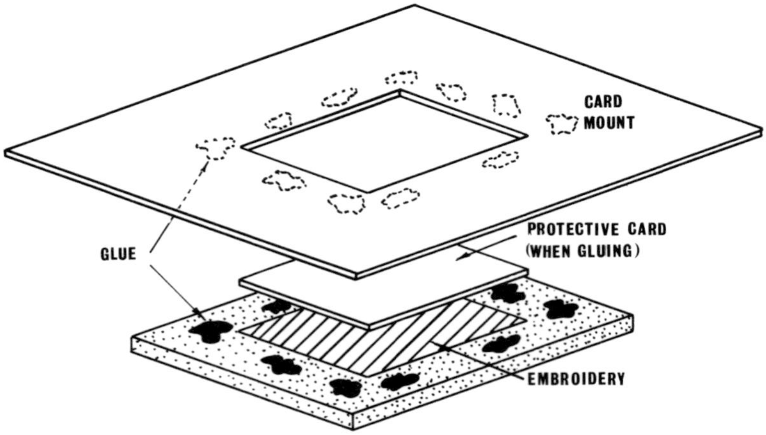

172 *The assembly of a card mount.*

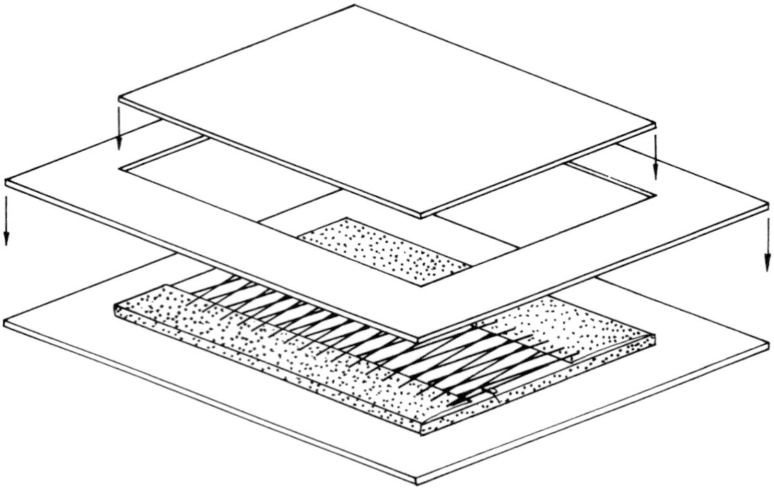

173 *Finishing the reverse side.*

firmly on the mount (which you should first protect with a sheet of paper, to avoid fingerprints).

6 Turn over the work, so that it now lies face downwards on a wooden board, which has been protected by a sheet of clean paper.

7 If you feel that the card mount needs strengthening to make it more rigid, then a piece of strawboard or old, damaged card, can be stuck to the back of the mount. To do this you need to cut out the shape of the plywood board, as this stands higher than the surface of the card. Stick this into position.

8 The surplus shape you have just cut out makes an ideal covering for the area of lacing and can be stuck into position using a contact glue *(173)*.

9 The entire back area will now be covered by 5 cm (2 in.) strips of brown sticky paper. Before you begin, however, you must first staple the card to the wooden board, along the outside edges; this is another reason why it is important to leave enough excess card. The card is stapled to the board at this stage in order to prevent it from buckling as the gummed paper is drying out.

10 Once the tape is completely dry, remove the staples and trim off the excess card to fit the frame size.

Glazing Glazing a piece of work is a matter of preference. I always have my own work glazed, as I feel it not only protects the embroidery from dust but also gives it a professional finish. If you do decide to have your embroideries glazed and framed, then it is worth having this done by a professional framer.

Double mounting using covered board The embroidery is stretched over a wooden frame as described earlier and stapled down. The edges of the frame can then be covered with ribbon, which is sewn on by hand. If possible, try to keep the join in the centre of the bottom edge, where it is not so easily seen. Do keep the joins away from the corner areas where they would be very noticeable.

You are going to mount the stretched embroidery onto another backing and for this you need a piece of chipboard approximately 5 cm (2 in.) bigger all round than the embroidery. Lay the embroidery panel in position on the chipboard and mark all round it with a pencil, then remove the embroidery.

You need to drill screw-holes into the board and the pencil lines should guide you to mark these in place. The holes are drilled at this stage so that you can easily determine the position of the screws.

The chipboard can now be treated in a number of different ways. It can be covered with plain or patterned fabric, which can be machine- or hand-embroidered, quilted or padded. Ribbons can be slip-stitched onto the fabric to form lines or geometric patterns, or the board can be painted instead of covered. The painting can be a simple all-over colour or an intricate design incorporating bound bands. However you decide to treat the board, remember that the central area will be covered by the embroidery and that this background should be part of a total image. It should be used to extend the design, complement or contrast with it, or simply form a subtle background to show off the embroidery.

Using the holes already drilled in the board, screw the two pieces together, until the embroidery is firmly held to the base mount. You must take care, however, to match the length of the screws to the thickness of the boards; if they are too long they will pierce the embroidery.

Finish off the edges by slip-stitching ribbon along the sides, or make a flat frame from thin slats of wood. Use slats which have first been painted or varnished, then nail into position with panel pins. Try to nail the pins slightly below the surface of the wood as this prevents any unsightly bumps. The hole made by the nail is filled in with a little wood filler, rubbed down with fine sandpaper and the paint or varnish is then touched in.

Double mounting with frames This method of mounting is an integral part of the technique and design of the embroidery. It consists of a deeper frame or series of frames covered with layers of open worked embroidery. It is viewed from the front, through layers of cutwork, pulled thread or drawn threadwork to the final opaque background. The effect is similar to that of a stage in a theatre, with its various scenic drops and backcloths.

The first layer of embroidery is very open and could consist, perhaps, of an arch of trees. This is stapled onto the front side of the frame, along the edge, *not* at the back, and any excess fabric is trimmed away. The second open layer is worked and stapled, again along the edge, but this time covering the back. Trim away any spare fabric. The final backcloth fabric, either plain, painted or machined, is placed behind the open second layer and stapled into place, along the edge *(174)*.

This technique could be developed using two or three frames, to give an enclosed box shape with stepped layers of fabric. Transparent fabrics such as organza would work very well on some of the layers, as they can be embroidered or cut away to create areas of texture or subtle delicacy. Scrim or fine open-weave fabrics would be suitable for drawn threadwork or pulled work. These could form the basis for the heavier shapes, especially when worked in machine embroidery, as the raw edges are easily covered and concealed, without the risk of fraying.

The successive frames can be screwed together and their edges finished off. Using the same principle as described in the previous paragraph, thin strips of painted or varnished wood can be nailed down with panel pins to cover the edges. Do ensure that the width of wood used as a covering is the same width as the edges to be covered.

Another method would be to cover card with fabric then stick down the card shapes over the exposed edges.

1 Cut four pieces of card to fit the frame size.

2 Position the card onto the fabric and cut out the shapes, allowing extra for turnings.

3 Cut out a small rectangle from each of the four corners, making sure that you do not cut right up to the card.

4 Turn in one of the shorter sides and glue down with a rubber-based adhesive. Repeat the process on the opposite side, pulling the fabric to give a smooth tight fit.

5 Repeat, using the same method along the sides, always gently pulling the fabric. Cover all four pieces of the card in the same way.

6 Stick the covered card shapes to the sides of the box using a contact glue.

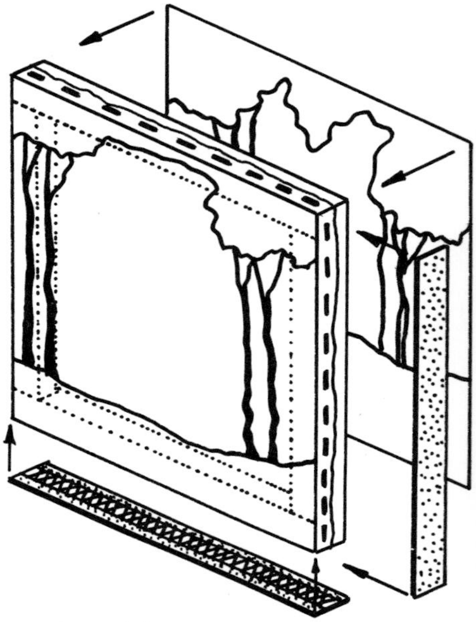

174 *Layered frames.*

Mount covered with fabric You may wish to cover your card mount with fabric, and this is a straightforward procedure.

1 Place the fabric on a flat, clean surface, with the wrong side facing uppermost. The card window mount can then be positioned on the fabric. Line up the edges of the card with the straight grain of the fabric and mark out its shape with tailor's chalk, being careful to hold the card in position. Leave a turning allowance of approximately 4–5 cm ($1\frac{1}{2}$–2 in.) and cut the shape. Try not to let the card slip.

2 Make a single cut into the inner corners, then apply the glue to the card a little way in from the edges and fold over the fabric, pressing down firmly to secure *(175)*.

3 When all the four turnings of the inner section have been stuck, the outer turnings are covered in the same way as the card rectangles described above.

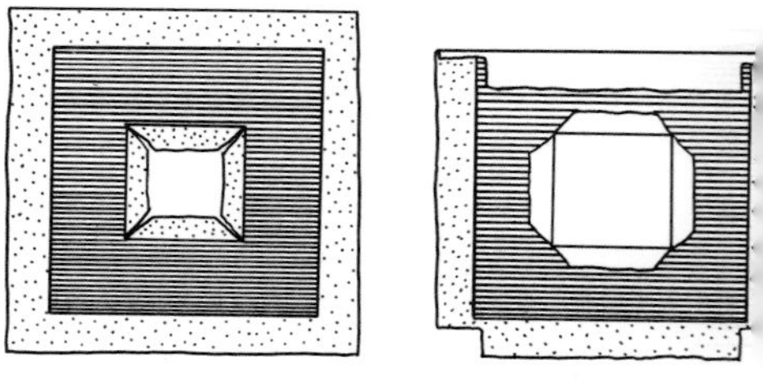

175 *Fabric-covered window mounts.*

4 Cut away the excess fabric from the corners. Apply glue to the card, slightly set back from the edge. Fold over the top turning, pulling gently to smooth out any wrinkles. Turn in the opposite side and repeat until all four sides are fixed.

Card mounts whose inner shapes are ovals, squares or arches can also be covered in this way *(176)*. The only difference is that where curves are indicated, the inner turnings need to be snipped at intervals around the curve.

Mounting irregular-shaped embroidery The instructions for the cutting of mounts has been confined to regular shapes made up of straight lines or curves which can easily be measured and drawn out. But you may want to mount an irregular-shaped embroidery, perhaps one with an outside band of couched thread where the corners are curved instead of angular.

To obtain a perfect fit, you must take an accurate tracing of the outside shape. Hold down the tracing paper with masking tape to prevent any movement and on the top side write 'top', to avoid getting it upside down or back to front at a later stage. Work on the reverse side of the card and lay the tracing face downwards on top of this. Secure the corners with masking tape and redraw over the traced lines, thereby marking the card with the imprint of the drawing.

Cut all curves first; if you have any straight lines, these can be cut with a ruler. You will need a steady hand and a strong wrist; do not try and rush, as free-hand cutting needs care and concentration. Once the card is cut, turn it over and fit to the embroidery.

As with all these methods, a little patience and care is needed to achieve a good finished result. Use the correct tools and adhesives and always double-check lines and measurements before making any cut, or sticking down any surface.

If you are glazing the work, make sure that the glass is clean and free from smears. Check that there are no loose threads lying on the surface of the work, otherwise they may drop and be trapped under the glass, possibly lodging in an unwanted and prominent position, which would necessitate the removal of the frame at a later date.

It is better to have a simple, well-cut mount than a complicated, badly put together one. If you are unable to cut mounts or matts, and I admit that a strong wrist is required, then it is better either to ask a competent friend or husband to cut it for you, or to take the job to your local framer. It is more expensive to have your work framed professionally, but the outlay is justified, especially if the piece is of importance, as it would be for an examination or for an exhibition, where presentation would be noticed.

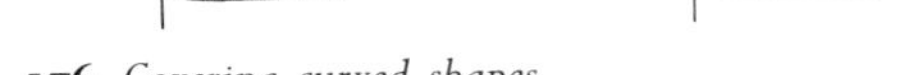

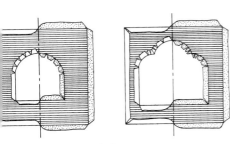

176 *Covering curved shapes.*

8 Work in progress

This section shows how a piece of my own work is developed from the initial idea, through the design and technical stages, to the finished piece. It also illustrates the practical use of the techniques covered in previous chapters.

The development of a piece of work demonstrates how essential each part of the process is to the whole, and it should also help you to understand the necessity of preliminary observation and paperwork.

CONCEPT AND DESIGN

The thumbnail sketches show a scene viewed from different angles and positions, roughly drawn in, showing the mass and proportion of land to sky *(177)*.

I find it helpful to enclose my sketches in boxes, as this contains the area of landscape to be drawn, and, especially if you are going to be working fast or wish to produce a lot of ideas on one sheet of paper, it will help to prevent them being jumbled together. Sketches which are not contained may look too confusing when you are away from the actual scene.

At this stage I want the landscape to dominate the picture, so my horizon line is placed high, in order to show more of the hills and fields. I am also interested in the way the hills fold into each other and how the fields follow their contours. They illustrate a variety of shapes, especially where some look as if they have been dissected into narrow strips. This makes an interesting feature within the landscape and could become a focal point of the design.

Once I have selected my view, I draw out a rough sketch on another sheet of paper *(178)*. This drawing is larger than the thumbnail sketches but is still not a detailed drawing. For this design, I am interested in the overall shape of the landscape so do not need a detailed drawing; I want an impression of the scene.

A diluted ink wash has been applied in some areas, and shows any change of direction within the field structure; for example, if a field has been ploughed or mown, then these new 'lines' do not necessarily follow the contours, but can cut horizontally or vertically across the field's surface.

DESIGN

Graph paper has been used to plan out the structure of the design *(179)*. This needs to be as accurate as possible, because a tracing for the stencil will be cut from it.

The landscape sketch has been transferred to the design and will be used as the main central section. Some minor changes have been made to the shapes of the hills, and more trees have been added to give textural interest, but I have decided to keep the landscape as near as possible to the original.

A feature of my work is the use of 'frames within frames', of seeing the same scene from different viewing perimeters, with extended hill lines connecting one plane to another; this design illustrates these features.

As I want to keep the central, landscape area as a representational scene, but also wish it to have more breadth and space as a design, I have extended the horizon line on the right-hand side, outwards from the picture plane, to the edge of the design. To balance the left side and give it a different viewing

177 *Rough sketches of landscape.*

178 *A selected view is colour-washed to give extra information for use in the studio.*

179 *The design planned out on graph paper.*

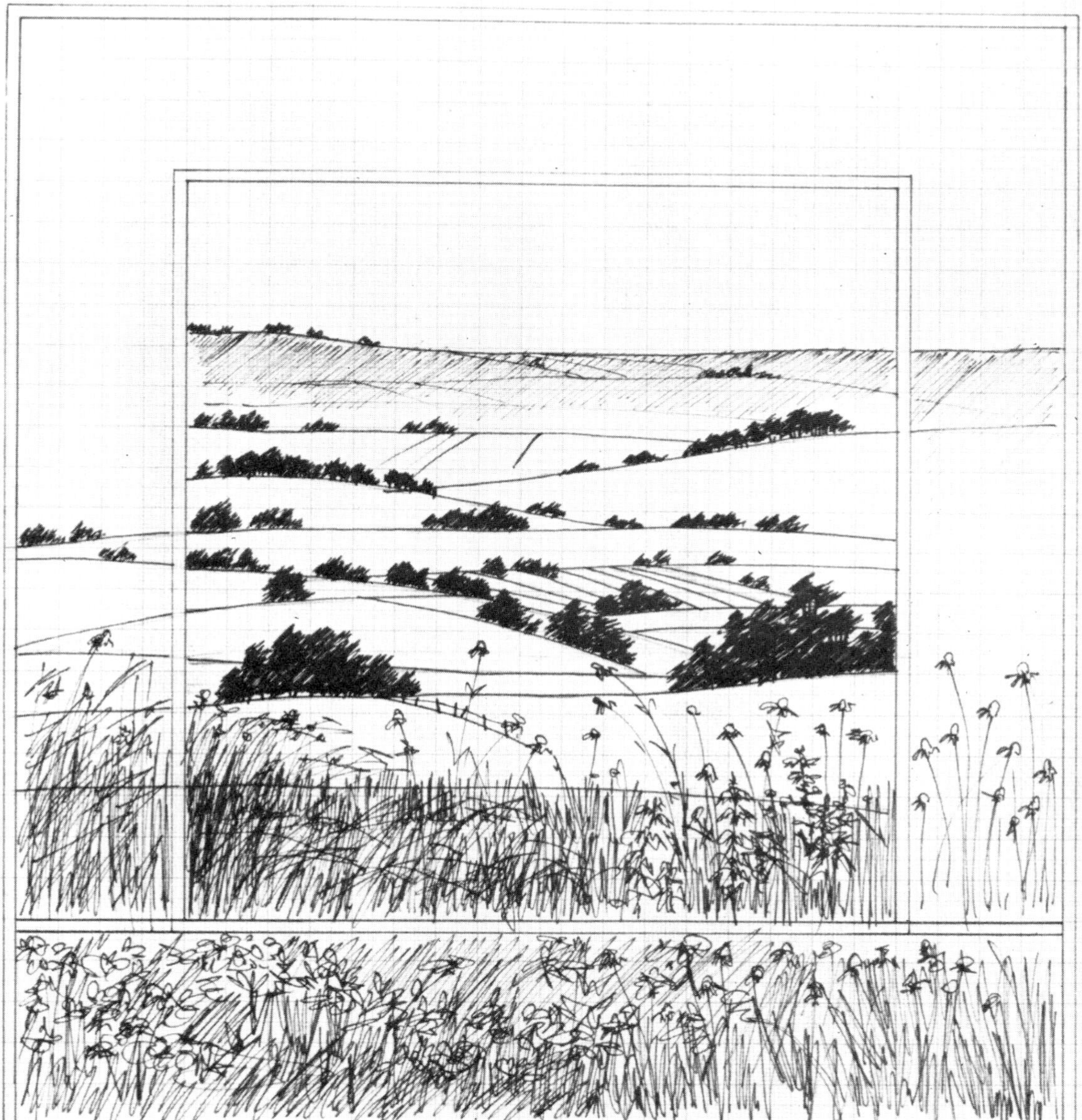

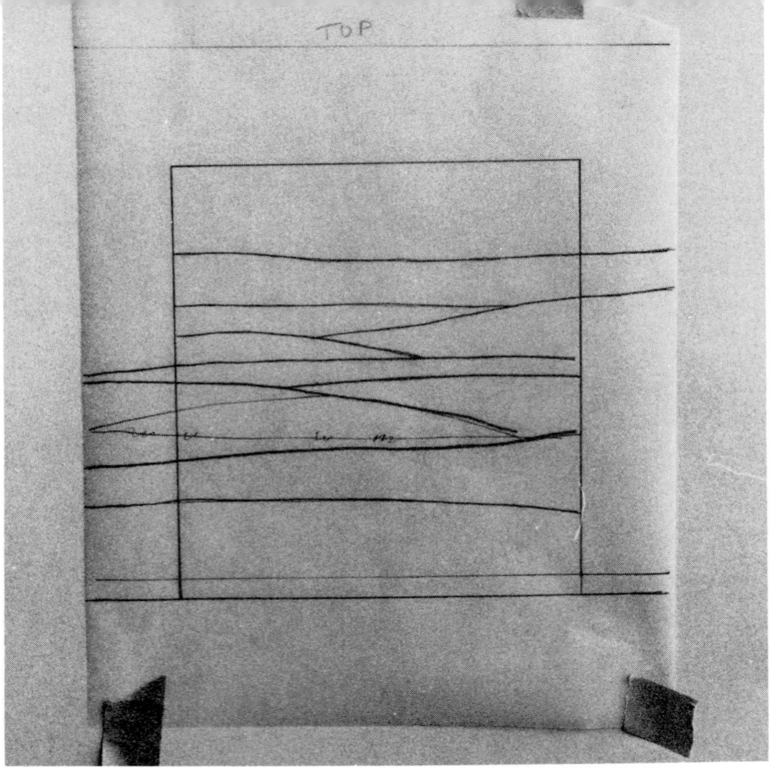

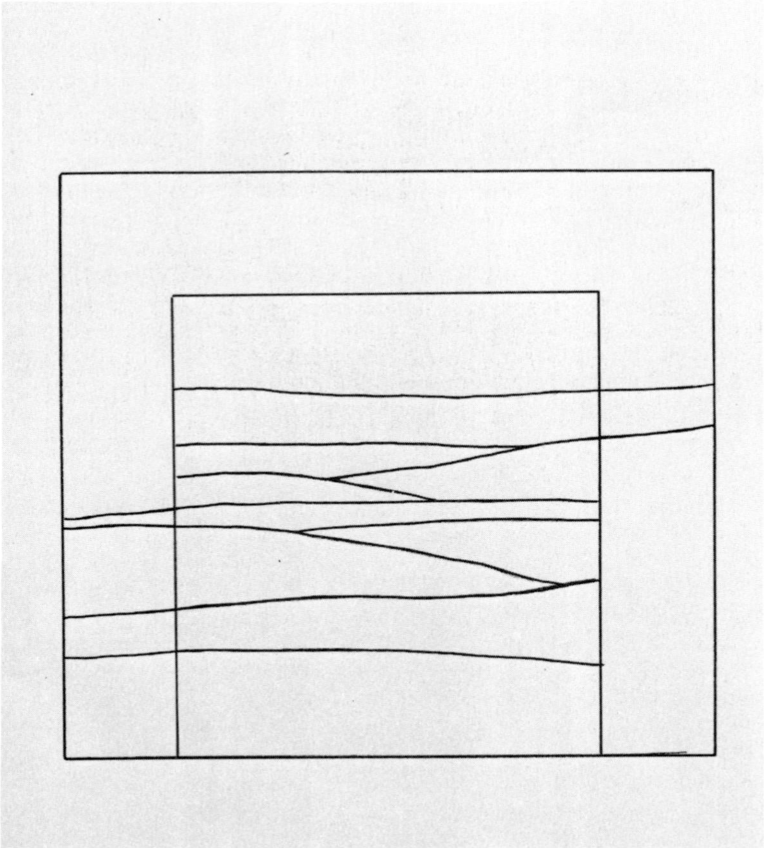

180a *A tracing is taken of the design.*

180b *The stencil is drawn out on cartridge paper.*

181 *Slubbed silk stretched diagonally to suggest slanting rain.*

interest, I have dropped the horizon to field level. This creates the spatial quality I want and also breaks up the geometry of the landscape.

The weight of texture will be within the bottom section of the design and will give solidity to the foreground. It will also bring that area forward, strengthening the illusion of standing on a hillside looking down over the valley and upwards to the hills.

APPLICATION OF COLOUR

A tracing has been taken of the design *(180a)* and from that, the cartridge-paper stencil has been cut *(180b)*. This stencil must be as accurate as possible, especially where the dividing lines lie, as I want to have a colour change between the outside bands and the inner landscape. If the stencil was inaccurate, then I could run the risk of overshooting the dyes, instead of stopping exactly where I wanted the colour to change. Small strips of double-sided tape have been stuck on the back of the stencil to prevent it from slipping when placed on the fabric.

I have used a piece of pale turquoise Honan silk (without a slub). I prefer to use the plain-weave silks, because I find that the slub weave has a tendency to pick up excess dye, which can ruin a delicate sprayed area, such as a sky. Slub weaves can be used to advantage, however, if you do want a textured surface. For instance, if the fabric is stretched so that the slub lies horizontally along the design, then its effect can be exaggerated with texture to suggest a field or moorland, where tufts of grass or heather stand out amongst the other grasses; but if it is stretched diagonally, then diagonal movements can be suggested, for example, slanting rain *(181)*. The silk is ironed to remove any creases, stretched over a flat, wooden frame and stapled down.

The paper stencil is positioned in place *(182a)*, the protective backing peeled off and the stencil is gently stuck to the surface of the fabric. (Do remember that the double-sided tape is only applied to the outside edges of the design, as its function is to prevent the stencil from slipping.)

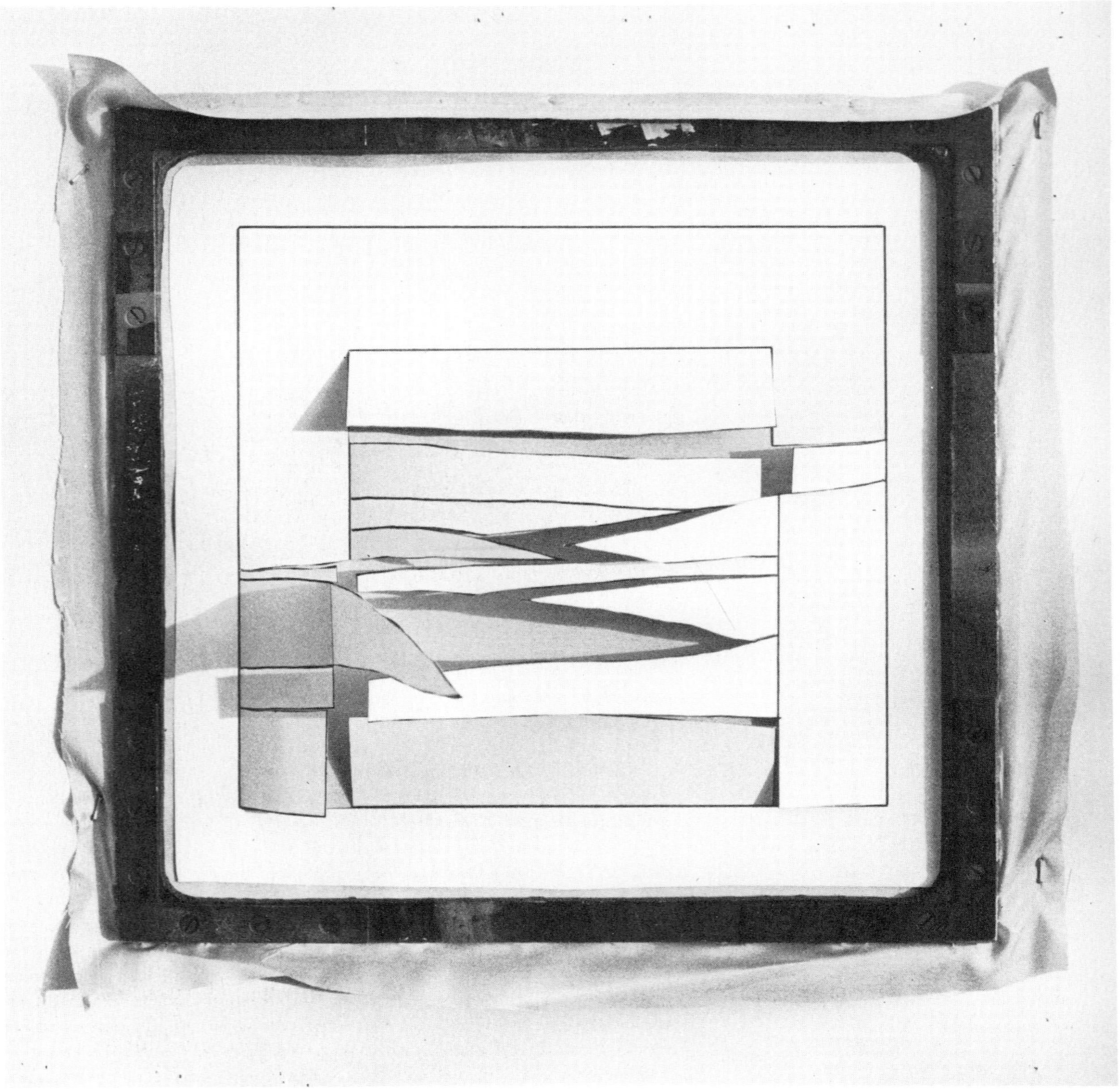

182a *The paper stencil in position on the frame.*

The dyes have been sprayed onto the fabric using a basic airbrush kit *(182b)*. Each colour is applied and then allowed to dry (using a hair-dryer to accelerate the process). The sprayed areas show simple planes of background colour, which will also act as guidelines when the texture is applied. The section containing the middle distance has more colour interest and also shows the fields, dissected into thin strips. This area of sprayed interest will eventually balance with the foreground texture.

A piece of clean paper has been laid on top of the dyed fabric, which is then ironed to remove any excess dye and also to fix the colours. Different dyes have different methods of fixing, so check the manufacturer's instructions.

182b *The background is sprayed with colour to suggest field planes.*

MACHINE EMBROIDERY

Initially I have machined in the hill and field lines, using the lighter, greyer colours for the distant horizon and hill lines. The colour of the threads gradually changes, so that the foreground lines are quite dark. In the same way, the textural masses of the trees intensify in colour as they near the fields in the front, so a more three-dimensional illusion is being created by simply changing the colours of the threads.

As I want this piece of work to give the impression of looking down over a valley and up to the opposite hills, I have added some grey-toned tree images *(183)*. This has the effect of 'lifting' the eye to the hill's horizon.

The intense areas of texture have been confined to the immediate foreground, suggesting grasses and flowers. Some of this texture has 'broken'

the front field line, where the flowers have penetrated other fields. Although this foreground texture has been allowed to break through into other areas, I have kept the detail below centre, emphasizing the illusion of recession.

To broaden the spatial atmosphere, the flowers have been extended to the outside borders; the texture continues on the left side of the picture, but there is a slight change of design on the right. Although the design has been changed, the continuity is achieved by the introduction of the daisy shape and colour. So the design of the right-hand border is open and spacious but the image of the flower, which is familiar to the scene, gives interest without the addition of new and possibly confusing imagery.

Hand embroidery in silk threads has also been added to the immediate foreground to illustrate the light and dark shades of the wind-blown grasses, and to lift the colour of the machine embroidery *(184)*.

183 *The hill lines and trees are machine embroidered.*

184 *More embroidery is added to the foreground to give interest and texture.*

The painted inset balances the weight of the composition, continues the colour of the grasses and flowers in the foreground and also gives another instance of surface interest, as a painted surface has a different quality to one which is embroidered.

The thin inner frames and bands are wrapped in silk thread, the colours chosen to blend in with the background tones *(185)*. I use these wrapped bands to form a link between the embroidery, the dyed fabric and the painting. This method also uses thread in a way not commonly associated with embroidery, for it combines the geometric frame with the richness and subtlety of pure silk threads.

185 *Silk-wrapped borders attached to the card (seen from the back).*

MOUNTING AND FRAMING

Once stretched, the embroidery is mounted in a simple card mount and because I did not wish to leave the inner edge white, this has been carefully painted with gouache, to match the colour of the card. The final stage is to glaze and frame the embroidery in a plain, gold moulding.

This book has set out to show that with a little observation and thought, embroidery can be an exciting medium through which to depict landscape and all its derivatives. Although I have specifically concentrated on machine embroidery, any technique may be used if the subject matter is good and the design is strong.

However much you enjoy working on your own, you may at some time find it

186 *The finished embroidery.*

necessary to seek help or advice, and for this reason I would suggest that some of the exercises could be carried out either with another embroidery friend, or within a group, as you will be able to receive and confer advice and constructive criticism. Above all, remember the importance of *looking*, because from this, all else stems.

SUPPLIERS

It is a good idea to write to suppliers before sending money, just to check that they are still trading and that addresses are still valid.

UK

Mary Allen
Wirksworth
Derbyshire DE4 4BN
Full range of DMC machine threads

Borovick Fabrics Ltd
16 Berwick Street
London W1V 4HP
Wide range of fabrics

Angela Carr
The Old Rectory
Bruntingthorpe
Leicestershire LE17 5NR
Fabric transfer paints

Coats Domestic Marketing Division
39 Durham Street
Glasgow G41 1BS
Full range of Anchor embroidery threads, information and lists of stockists

John Lewis
Oxford Street
London W1
Large range of sewing threads and fabrics, machine needles and accessories

Mace and Nairn
89 Crane Street
Salisbury
Wiltshire SP1 2PY
General embroidery supplies

Christine Riley
53 Barclay Street
Stonehaven
Kincardineshire AB3 2AR
General embroidery supplies

Terry Taylor Associates
27 Woodland Road
Tunbridge Wells
Kent TN4 9HW
Silk fabrics and fabric paints

George Weil & Sons Ltd
63–65 Riding House Street
London W1P 7PP
Deka Permanent and Deka Silk, fabric paints for painting and spraying

Whaleys Ltd
Harris Court
Great Horton
Bradford
West Yorkshire BD7 4EQ
Many different types of fabric

USA

Appleton Brothers of London
West Main Road
Little Compton
Rhode Island 02837

American Thread Corporation
90 Park Avenue
New York

The Thread Connection
1020 East Carson Street
Pittsburgh
Pennsylvania 15203

Threadbenders
2260 Como Avenue
St Paul
Minnesota 55108

The Thread Shed
307 Freeport Road
Pittsburgh
Pennsylvania 15215

INDEX